THE SECOND Tonia Todman COLLECTION

Other books published by Tonia Todman

The Tonia Todman Collection (Book 1)
Tonia Todman's Papermaking Book
Tonia Todman's Stenciling Book
Tonia Todman's Heirloom Sewing Book
Tonia Todman's Wreaths & Garlands Book
Tonia Todman's Candlewicking Book

Published by Sally Milner Publishing

THE SECOND *Tonia Todman* COLLECTION

SALLY MILNER

First published in 1994 by
Sally Milner Publishing Pty Ltd
558 Darling Street
Rozelle NSW 2039 Australia

Reprinted in 1994 (twice)

Design by Gatya Kelly, Doric Order
Photography by Andrew Elton
Illustrations and pattern sheet by Lesley Griffith
Typeset in Australia by Asset Typesetting Pty Ltd
Printed in Australia by Impact Printing, Melbourne

National Library of Australia
Cataloguing-in-Publication data:

Todman, Tonia.
The second Tonia Todman collection
ISBN 1 86351 127 X.

1. Handicraft. I. Title. (Series: Milner craft series)

745.5

Contents

Acknowledgements
Foreword 1
Austrian Blinds 2
Applying Lace to Smocked Baby's Gown 5
Bride's Flower Circlets 6
Calico Angel 7
Calico Bear 8
Candlewicked Bear 10
Candlewick Embroidery Sachets 12
Cardboard Carton Doll's House 17
Coiled Place Mats 18
Craft Coiling 19
Decal-trimmed Garden Tools 20
Decorating with String, Rope, Raffia and Shells 21
Docile Dinosaurs 22
Easy Découpage 23
Easy Director's Chair Cover 24
Fabric Draught Stoppers 26
Fairy Wand, Wings and Skirt 27
Fireplace Screen 29
Floor Treatments 31
Frilled Cushion Covers 33
Garden or Tool Apron 34
Garland Country-style 35
Greetings Cards 37
Ideas on How to Decorate Hats 38
Inexpensive, Practical and Quick-to-make Christmas Presents and Decorations 39
Interfacing 40
Jigsaw Blocks 41
Kids' Crafts 42
Lined Picnic Basket 44
Lucinda Bunny 46
Make Your Own Bedlinen 51
Old-fashioned Changing Screen 53

Painted Pots for All Seasons 54
Painting on Silk 55
Paper-covered Pencils and Container 56
Paper Pricking 57
Picture Frames 58
Pleated Paper Lampshades 59
Pomanders 60
Pot-pourri-filled Bow 61
Preserved Flowers 62
Raffia Doll in Corn Dolly Style 64
Ragging and Sponging Techniques for Walls or Wooden Surfaces 65
Scrunchies 67
Shell-covered Picture Frame and Box Top 68
Silk Pearl Bag 69
Small Bear in a Bag 71
Small Christmas Puddings 74
Smocked Baby's Gown 75
Soft Leather Baby Slippers 80
Soft-toy Making 82
Stencilled Quilt 83
Stiffened Fabric Ideas 87
Sweet Hearts for Children's Parties 90
Tapestry 92
Tie-on Director's Chair Cover 93
Tissue-box Cover 94
Tonia's Country Rabbits 95
Travel Pillow 96
Trimming Sandshoes 97
Tying a Bow Around Something 98
Tying a Bow to Fasten onto Something 100
Valance or Gathered Pelmet 102
Vera the Virtuous Vine Tamer 103
Wheat Heart 104
Wired Roses and Rose Buds 105
Woollen Blanket for Baby 107
Zipper 112

Acknowledgements

Thank you to the many hard-working craft suppliers and importers who have so generously supported me over the years. May we continue to travel together!

Birch Haberdashery
Ceramic Hobbies
DMC Threads
Jo Sonja Paints
John Boyle and Co
Just Craft
Liberty of London
Lincraft
Pioneer Craft
Ray Toby Fabrics
Simplicity Patterns

Thank you, too, to all my friends at Channel Ten — especially Bert Newton. Their unstinting support, good humour and encouragement is typical of a totally professional and delightful group — and they are certainly that!

List of Colour Plates

Plate 1: Frilled cushion cover; silk flower-decorated hat.

Plate 2: Decorating with string, rope, raffia and shells.

Plate 3: Small bear, with and without a bag.

Plate 4: Woollen blanket for baby, with grub roses detail.

Plate 5: Vera the virtuous vine tamer, decal-trimmed garden tools.

Plate 6: Smocked baby's gown with greetings card; smocked baby gown details, (a) drawn-up gathers ready for embroidery, (b) detail of grub roses and smocking, (c) smocking with French knot trim.

Plate 7: Smocking detail.

Plate 8: Tonia's country rabbits.

Plate 9: Stiffened fabric bows.

Plate 10: Pot-pourri-filled bow.

Plate 11: Lined picnic basket.

Plate 12: Trimmed sandshoes.

Plate 13: Fairy wand, wings and skirt.

Plate 14: Docile dinosaurs.

Plate 15: Painting on silk.

Plate 16: Stencilled floor treatment.

Plate 17: Garland country-style.

Plate 18: Christmas presents and decorations.

Plate 19: Lucinda bunny and embroidery detail.

Plate 20: Stencilled quilt.

Plate 21: Coiled place mats.

Plate 22: Basket trimmed with stiffened fabric bow.

Plate 23: Easy découpage.

Plate 24: Jigsaw blocks.

Back cover: *Left to right:* Easy director's chair cover; shell-covered boxes: stiffened bow-covered frame and fabric-covered tissue box.

Foreword

As the pace of the craft industry in Australia continues to increase, so, it seems, does my work output! I've gathered together more of your favourite crafty ideas from television, this time with more pictures and illustrations, to help and encourage those just beginning to take an interest in craft, and those who are dedicated crafts-people. Those of you who regularly watch me fall about laughing with my dear friend Bert Newton on his show *Good Morning Australia* (while attempting to convey some crafty idea) or who watch the highly successful show *Healthy, Wealthy and Wise* for more of my craft and decorating ideas, will know I have a keen sense of practicality and budgets. Good design, a sound purpose and a charming appearance are always the things I look for in crafty items — and I'm sure you'll find plenty of these to tempt you within these pages.

Austrian Blinds

The beauty of these blinds is that precise measurements are not crucial to the look of the finished product. They work on the principle of the blind moving up and down over fine, strong cords that are threaded through rings on guiding tapes. Fabric choices are many — providing the fabric is not too heavy. Consider calico — blinds look wonderful in this all-purpose cotton fabric. Austrian blinds do require fullness of fabric to look effective, and you need to consider whether or not to line them. Consider the impact a print fabric will have when viewed from the outside of your house — it may be better to line it with a neutral fabric similar in colour to curtain lining. I suggest you read through the instructions before starting.

Considerations

Decide whether or not to line the blind. Determine how many cords you wish it to have; this in turn will tell you how many scallops you'll have across the bottom. Do you wish to have a frill around the edge? Also consider the blind's means of support. A metal or wooden rod supported by two or three brackets is commonly used and is efficient. (See notes below on how to measure for cord, tape and small hooks.)

Materials

To measure for main fabric

Measure the width and depth of the window to be covered. Allow for at least double the width and double the depth. Piece fabric strips using flat seams to achieve fabric of these dimensions. Take care to match patterns where necessary. If you wish to line your blind (it will tend to sit better if you do, especially if you choose a lightweight textile for your main fabric), allow for the same amount of pieced lining fabric as that of your main fabric piece.

If you wish to have a frill around the sides and base of the blind, allow for a 22 cm (8¾″) wide strip that is double the measurement of both sides and the base of your blind fabric piece. If you are lining the blind, cut a main fabric strip 11 cm (4½″) wide, and a strip of lining, both the same length as above.

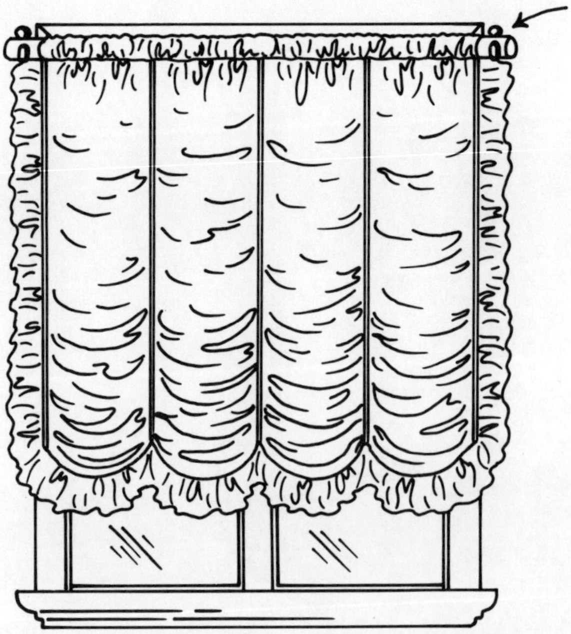

To measure for cord, tape and hooks

You will require a minimum of three rows of tape per blind. The tape comes with small guiding rings for the cord attached, or with small fabric loops through which the cord travels, or with pockets through which you thread rings for the cord. Purchase whichever you prefer. Tape length is the total of strips of tape you decide to stitch to your blind. For example, if you have four strips of tape, each 1.5 m (5′) long, you will need to purchase 6 m (20′) of tape. Cord length is the total length of tape, plus sufficient cord to travel from the top of each tape across to one side of the blind. You will need a screw-in ring hook for each tape, plus one more, and a cleat around which you will wind the cords to secure the blind at the desired level. You may also wish to purchase a bell-shaped cover to conceal the end-knot of the cords. See the illustration and all will become clear — it only sounds complicated.

Method

To make and attach frill to lined or unlined blinds

If you are adding a frill to a lined blind, make and attach this first. Place the frill strips together with right sides facing and edges matching. Stitch along one long edge, turn to right side, press stitched edge neatly. Turn in edges of short ends and stitch across. Gather remaining long edge. If not lining your blind, fold frill strip over double, press, finish short ends and gather raw edges. Measure the circumference of your support rod and add 3 cm (1¼″). Measure down from the top corners of the blind and mark this measurement. Starting and finishing at these points, pin and then stitch the gathered frill to the edge of main fabric piece, down sides and across lower edge, having right sides facing and edges matching. Neaten the frill raw edge if your blind is to be unlined.

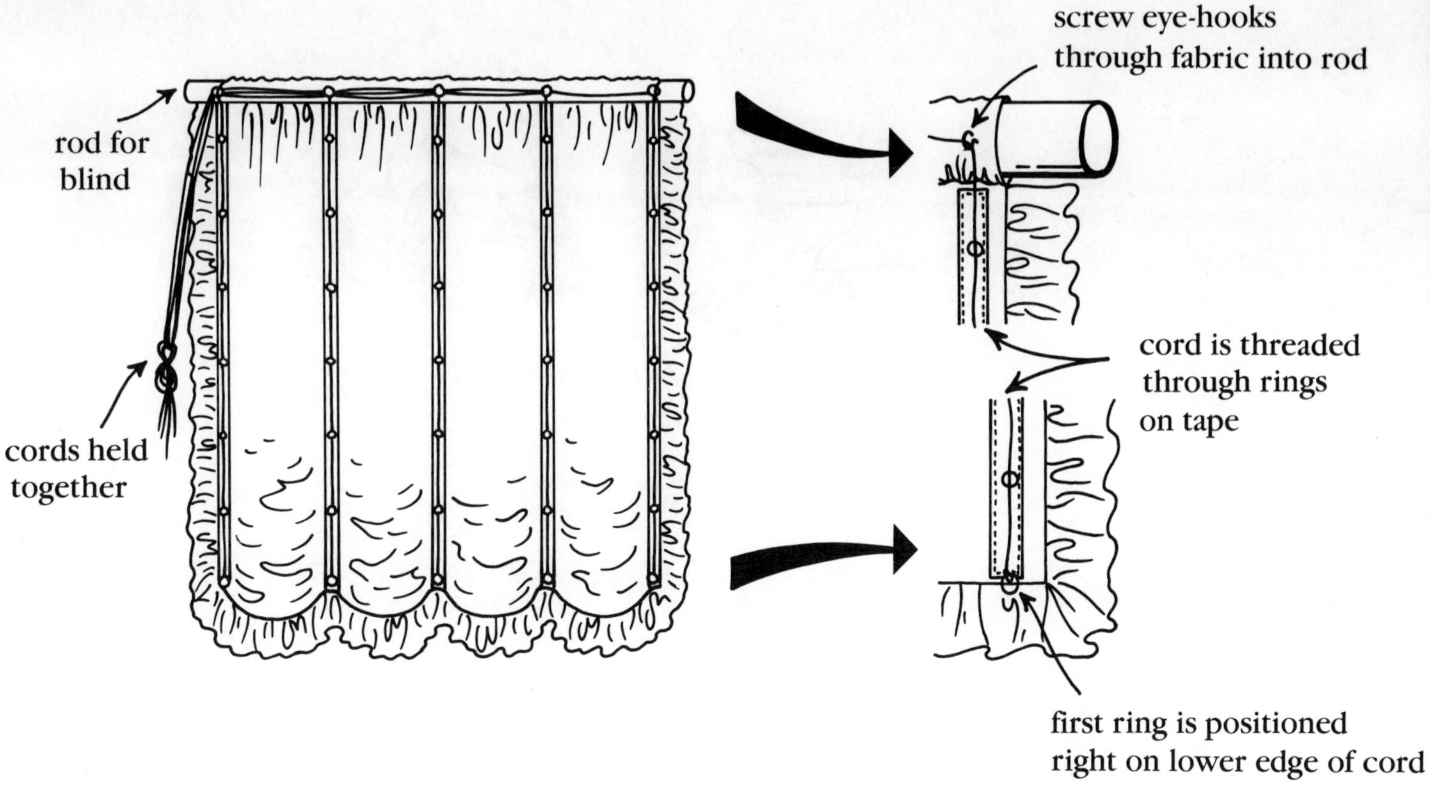

To line the blind

This is done before any cords are attached or rod casings made. Place the lining piece over the trimmed main piece, right sides facing and raw edges matching. Stitch down sides from the top and across lower edge — following previous stitching — through all thicknesses. Turn blind to right side, press carefully. If not attaching frill but still lining blind, omit any reference to frills and attach the lining to the main fabric in the above method. Continue to make casing (see below), and add tapes and cords as instructed.

Unlined blind

Make as for lined blind, omitting any reference to lining.

To make casing

Mark stitching lines and turn over top edge 1 cm (½″), then turn folded edge down to meet point where frill commences. If not attaching frill, measure the circumference of your support rod and add 3 cm (1¼″). Measure down from the top corners of the blind and mark this measurement. Stitch across blind through folded edge.

Stitch lengths of evenly spaced tapes onto blind, starting at lower edge with a ring, and finishing underneath casing stitching. Thread cords through rings on tape, tying ends of cords to lower ring, and being sure to allow extra to travel across to the edge of the blind.

To assemble

Thread rod through blind casing, then attach to support brackets. Adjust gathers evenly across rod, and mark tape positions on window frame. Screw in ring hook at each tape position, and one more to the side through which all cords will pass. Thread cords through ring hooks. Thread cords through knot-cover (if using) and tie ends of cords evenly into a knot. Slide cover down over knot. Find a suitable height for the cleat and attach to one side of the window frame.

Applying Lace to Smocked Baby's Gown

1. Place lace just in from fabric edge, right sides facing.
2. Turn your machine to a medium-width zig-zag and stitch so that the needle swings over the fabric edge and back into the edge of the lace.
3. The tension of stitches will tighten, drawing the fabric edge close to the lace and forming a small ridge. Press on right side of work.

Bride's Flower Circlets

The bases of these circlets are both the same; only the trimming and the way it is attached is different.

Materials for base

- *Three or four chenille-type pipe cleaners. If these are not available, substitute ordinary pipe cleaners and use greater quantities*
- *Satin ribbon for wrapping around pipe cleaners*
- *Sewing thread and needle, or quick-drying glue, or glue gun*

Materials for fresh-flower trim

- *A quantity of fresh flowers*
- *1 cm (½") wide satin ribbon or florist's tape*

Materials for ribbon rose trim

- *Quantity of ribbon roses (see Ribbon Roses)*
- *Quantity of extra 3 mm (⅛") wide satin ribbon tied into bows*
- *Hot-melt glue gun*

Method

To make base

Twist the ends of two pipe cleaners to bind them securely. Add more pipe cleaners to make up length required to encircle your head. Once you have the correct size, twist the ends of cleaners together to create a firm fit. Wind ribbon around cleaners until they are completely covered. Glue or stitch ends of ribbon to secure.

To trim with fresh flowers

The flower stems should be 4-5 cm (2") long. Position the first flowers so that the stems lie along the pipe cleaner base and wind the ribbon or tape (ribbon is more attractive) around stem and circlet. Place the next round of flowers over stems of preceding flowers, so that heads are close together. Wind stems to the circlet in the same manner as before.

Continue with this process until the circlet is completely covered with flowers. Spray with a fine mist of water and keep moist and cool until time to wear. Fasten with hair pins if necessary, although it is good to have the circlet coming down slightly onto the forehead — it won't fall off from this position.

To trim with ribbon roses

Have ready many ribbon roses and small bows tied from 3 mm (⅛") wide ribbon. Bind roses around circlet, with the bows tucked in and glued among them. The circlet must be completely covered with the trimmings.

These circlets look particularly pretty on bridesmaids. Dried flowers can be substituted for ribbon roses.

Calico Angel

Materials

- *About 60 cm (24″) of calico*
- *About 3 m (10′) of wide gold or Christmas ribbon, and about 3 m (10′) of a similar narrower ribbon. You may wish to use wire-edge ribbon for the back bow so that the ribbon loops resemble wings.*
- *A ping-pong ball*
- *Handful of sphagnum moss or reindeer moss*
- *A bunch of silk roses, sprayed gold, or ribbon roses*
- *Narrow ribbon for hanging, or cord*
- *Hot melt glue, or PVA glue*

Method

Tear the calico into 2 cm-wide (1″) strips, leaving a 10 cm-wide strip remaining untorn.

Fold in the edges of the wide strip and fold it over and over until it's about 20 cm (8″) long. Fold it over in half, enclosing about 10 strips of calico. These become the arms. Tie the folded wide strip around with another strip of calico to secure. Thread three 30 cm-long (12″) ribbon strips through over the calico strips, and tie narrow ribbon around the 'wrists' to secure.

Find the halfway point of the remainder of the calico (about 15–20 strips) and place this at the top of the folded piece (the shoulders), allowing the strips to fall to the front and the back. Place three strips of ribbon over the calico at the 'shoulders' and tie narrow ribbon around the Angel's waist to secure them. You may wish to place a dot of glue under the ribbons here and at the shoulders to secure them.

Glue small tufts of moss around the ping-pong ball (the head) to simulate hair. Twist the wire stems of the roses into a continuous chain of about six to eight flowers and secure these into a circular shape. Glue this garland around the head. Glue the head onto the shoulders, pressing it down well.

Tie ribbon around the waist again and into a large bow to resemble wings at the back. Tie narrow ribbon around the waist and into a loop for hanging.

Pull the ends of the calico arm strips to push up the ribbon strips and so give some fullness near the shoulders. Trim the ends of all calico strips at an angle, to any length you wish. Greater fullness and precision can be obtained if you press and starch each calico strip before starting the Angel.

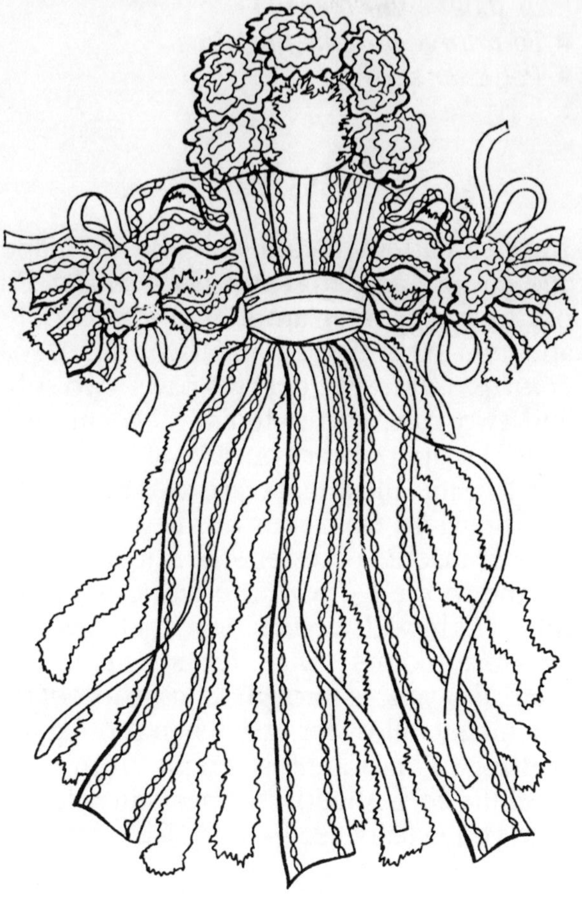

Calico Bear

This bear is very simply constructed, as the body and head pieces are cut all in one. A good bear for beginners!

Materials

- *70 cm (28") of 115 cm-wide (45") calico, or similar*
- *20 cm (8") of contrasting fabric*
- *2 safety eyes (if this bear is for an adult, you may wish to substitute two dark-coloured, dome-shaped buttons for eyes)*
- *Longest doll needle available*
- *Embroidery thread for facial features*
- *Linen thread dental floss for joints (linen thread available at haberdashery counter as shoe repair thread)*
- *Four large buttons for joints*
- *Polyester stuffing*

Method

Transfer pattern pieces onto brown paper and cut out pattern. *From plain fabric:* Cut out four legs, four arms, two front bodies and two back bodies and two ears. *From contrast fabric:* Cut out two paws, two soles and two ears, and a 10 cm x 94 cm (4'') x 38'') strip for bear's neck bow.

All seam allowances are 6–8 mm (¼'') (or the width from your needle to the edge of your machine presser foot is ideal — line up the foot edge with the fabric edge and this width will occur). Stitch curves and pressure points twice for strength. Clip seam allowances through to just short of the stitching to allow for ease when turning and stuffing. For added strength, turn your machine to a slightly shorter stitch length than you usually use — say 1¾–2.

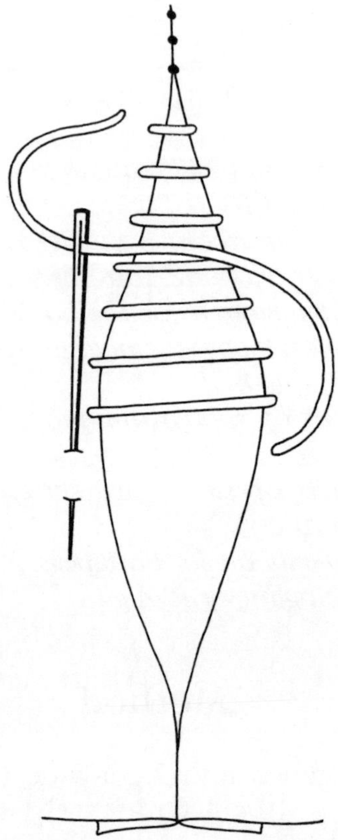

Ladder stitch for joining seams in soft toys

Step 1

Mark in the darts on the wrong side of the head, and the facial features on the front pieces — see illustrated pattern pieces. Mark in the darts on the lower back body. Mark where ears are to be stitched. Place plain ears together with contrasting fabric ears, and legs together in pairs. Noting illustration, pin paws onto ends of arms. It does not matter onto which end of the arm you pin the paws — they are identical.

Step 2

Sew the darts at the top of the body fronts, and press the darts downwards. Sew the body front sections together at the centre front. Stitch around the curved edge of the ears. Clip seams and turn to right side. Stuff ears with a very small amount of fibre. Baste ears into position on fronts at markings, matching raw edges.

Step 3

Stitch darts in the lower body backs, pressing open the dart seam allowances. Stitch body back sections together, leaving an opening for stuffing in centre back. Ease stitch around the back lower body with a gathering stitch. With right sides facing and edges matching, pin body back and front together, pulling up ease-stitching to fit front to back. Stitch around edges, then turn out to right side through stuffing opening. Fold neck tie over double lengthways, raw edges matching. Cut each end at an angle and stitch around the raw edges, leaving an opening in the centre for turning. Turn, press edge seam neatly.

Step 4

Press paws down onto arms. Place arms together in pairs and stitch around edges, leaving opening at upper arm back for turning and stuffing. Clip seams and turn to right side. On leg pairs stitch from toes around to heels, leaving an opening at upper back for turning and stuffing. Do not stitch across straight lower edge. Tie off stitching at toes and heels securely. Clip around straight lower foot edges at 1 cm (½″) intervals, to a depth just short of your seam allowance. Pin the soles to these clipped edges, fanning out the leg seam allowance to fit. When satisfied with fit, stitch and turn legs out to right side.

Step 5

Push domed button part of eyes through front at markings — you may have to snip through the fabric very slightly to do this. Connect the safety ring to each eye by pushing the ring over the shaft of each eye. The points at the centre of the safety ring face away from the dome. If using buttons, sew these on later. Stuff legs, arms and body with fibre. Take your time doing this, making sure bear is firmly stuffed and is not lumpy or uneven. When complete, close stuffing openings by hand with small stitches (see illustration of ladder stitch) using double thread in your needle.

Step 6

Thread linen thread onto the long needle and knot ends together. Take a small stitch to secure ends at one arm or leg 'X' on the body. Take the thread through and back through the button, then take the needle and thread through the body at the 'X' and out at the opposite 'X'. Stitch through and back through the opposite button, then take the needle back through the body and complete the first button, pulling the thread very firmly. Take the needle back through the body again and complete the second button, securing the thread under the second button. Repeat this process with the remaining two limbs and buttons. Be sure to stitch these limbs on securely as your bear will come in for a lot of love and attention!

Step 7

Stitch on eyes using double thread and your long needle, pulling the thread from one eye to the other, causing small indentations which will give your bear's face some shape. Using three strands of embroidery thread, use satin stitch to make the nose and small chain stitches to make the mouth smile. Tie the neck tie around your bear's neck and into a bow.

Safety note. If you do allow a small child to play with this bear, please be sure to stitch on limbs and any other trimming strongly and with extreme care, to avoid accidents.

Candlewicked Bear

This is a very easy bear to make, as his head and body are all in one. Limbs are all sewn in rather than jointed, and you can let your creative spirit free when embroidering him as he lends himself very well to all sorts of candlewicking embellishment. I suggest that it would be almost impossible to embroider him too much! I've made him from a seeded calico or muslin, though bears of other plain colours would be equally handsome, and you may use either French or colonial knots to embellish him.

Colonial knots

Materials

- *60 cm (24") of 115 cm-wide (45") fabric*
- *Candlewick embroidery thread*
- *Button eyes (if desired)*
- *Polyester fibre stuffing*

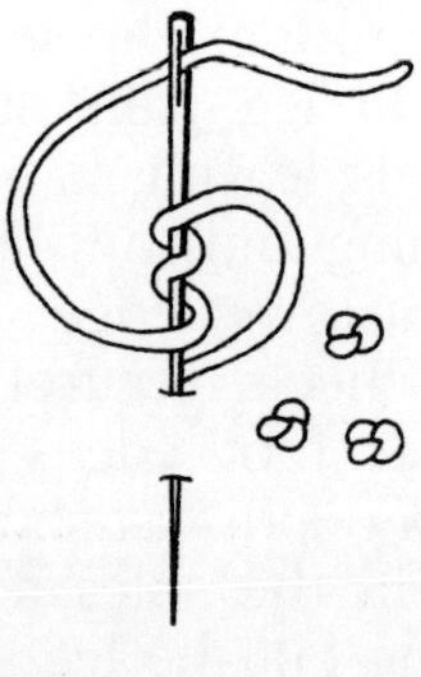

French knots

Method

Note: Stitch curves twice for strength and clip into corners and around curves for ease.

Trace off the pattern pieces shown on the pattern sheet at the back of the book. Cut four ears, four legs, two soles, four arms, two front body pieces and two back body pieces — 6 mm (¼″) seams are allowed.

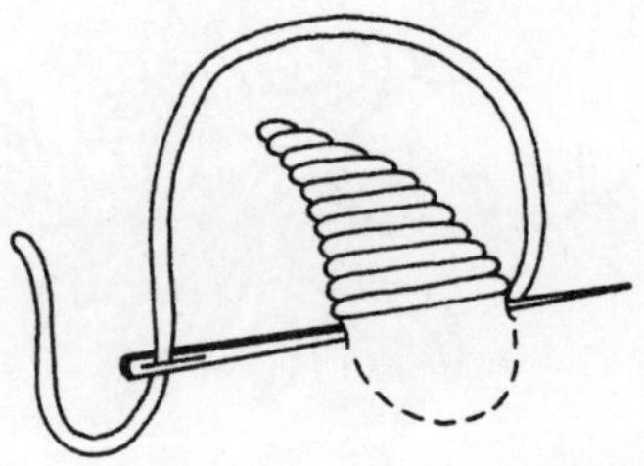

Satin stitch

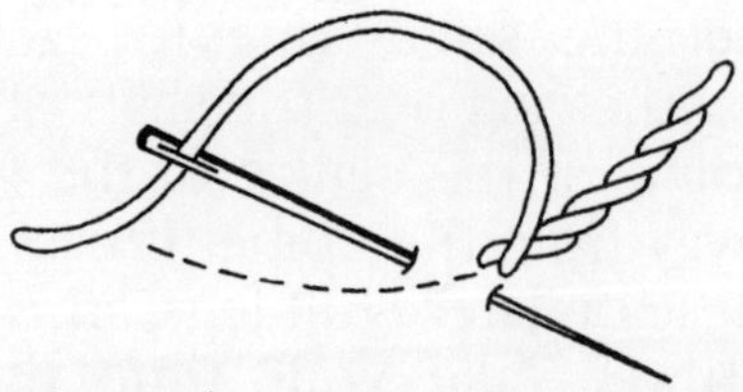

Stem stitch

Stitch the darts in the ears, the back and front heads, the legs and the arms. Place the ears together in pairs and stitch around curved edge. Turn and press.

Place legs together in pairs and, leaving sole open, stitch up front and up back seams of legs, leaving an opening in the back for stuffing, and leaving open the top edges. Clip around the sole edge of the foot to a depth just short of 6 mm (¼″) and pin, then stitch, the sole to this edge, right sides facing and raw edges matching. Fan out the seam allowance of the leg to make this easier. Turn legs to right side. Place the arms together in pairs and stitch around, leaving open the top straight edges and an opening in the back of the arm for stuffing. Turn to right side.

Place the front and back bodies together in pairs and stitch down centre back and centre front, leaving an opening in the centre back for stuffing.

Flatten the arms and the legs so that the seams align at the centre. The darts in the arms and legs should not be on the outside edge. Pin the arms and legs into position on the front piece, as marked on the pattern. Fold the arms and legs into the centre of the body and pin to keep them out of the way of machine stitching.

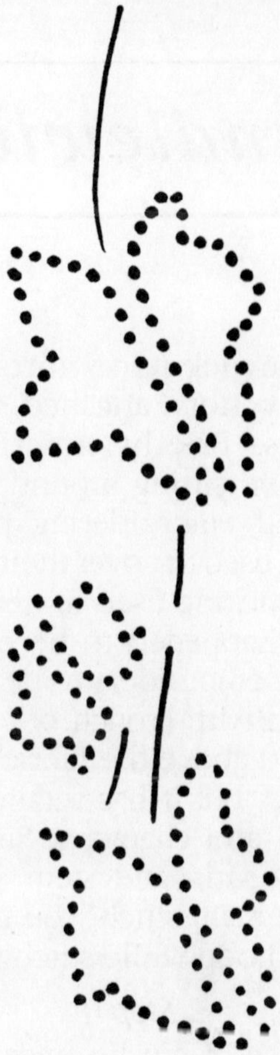

Pin the ears to the front head, aligning the darts in the ears with darts in the upper head. Place the body back over the body front, right sides facing and raw edges matching, and pin into place. Stitch around the body. Turn the bear inside out through the opening in the body back.

Stuff the legs, arms, then the body, with polyester fibre, closing the openings using ladder stitch and double thread. To avoid tangles in your sewing thread, place the end of the thread that comes off the needle first into your needle first, then knot the ends.

Embroider your bear using knots and stem stitch around the soles, ears, the body, paws and face. Stitch in your bear's nose, eyes and smile using satin stitch for the nose and chain stitch for the smile. Make three long 'lashes' fan out from each eye with simple straight stitch. Add button eyes if desired (button eyes need to be very securely attached if a child has the bear as a toy).

Candlewick Embroidery Sachets

Candlewicking embroidery has a lovely story attached to its beginnings. Briefly, American pioneer women, while sitting around their fires at night, started embroidering pieces of the heavy calico used to cover their wagons with the cotton wicking used in making candles. Both items happened to be cream and, in order for the embroidery to be felt and seen, they stitched with French or colonial knots as they stood above the fabric. Today it has been refined, but it has retained its homespun charm and character. Simple stitches are used — satin and stem stitches, with knots as the main stitch. You should use an embroidery hoop while stitching.

Step 1

On one piece of muslin trace off the three designs, leaving sufficient space between them for using your hoop. To trace, place the designs under the fabric and draw the patterns using a soft, sharp lead pencil. Any lead markings that remain visible after embroidery is complete can be rubbed away using an eraser.

Step 2

As a guide, use the following stitches to embroider the patterns — see page 10:
Stem stitch for any stem or curved line. *French knots* where any small, round, knot-like marking appears, and clustered close together in the centre of flowers and the buds, and borders. *Satin stitch* for the bud bases and flower petals. Use two strands of thread for the French knots and satin stitch, and a single strand for the stem stitch. You may like to use three strands for the border knots — try it and see if you like the thicker knots here.

Step 3

When embroidery is complete, cut out the sachets along the outer straight line. 6 mm (¼″) seam allowances are included. Cut out identical shapes from the remaining piece of muslin. Place the two pieces with right sides together and stitch around the edges, leaving a space for turning. Clip curved seams for ease and turn the sachets to the right side.

Step 4

Stuff the sachets with polyester fibre stuffing or pot-pourri, being sure they are evenly stuffed, and hand stitch closed the opening. Join the ends of the lace using a French seam, or be sure to overcast the raw edges well. For the heart, pin the half-way mark of the lace. For the circle and the square, pin the lace into quarters. Fold the circular sachet into quarters and pin the positions at the edge.

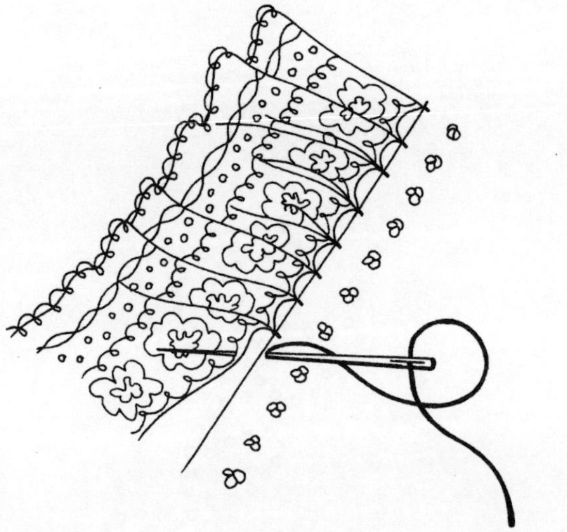

How to apply lace to the edge of candlewicked sachets

Step 5

Pin the lace onto the sachets matching the quarter or half points, butting the edge of the lace with the seam line. Pin the lace also at approximate quarter points on the heart. Note the illustration for stitching the lace. Thread a single strand of candlewick thread through a sharp needle and knot the end. Hold your work so that the seam edge sits vertically away from you. Bring the needle through the seam edge, from back to front. Take a stitch back through the fabric beside where the needle emerged and under the edge of the lace. Bring the needle back to the seam edge at the entry point and take a small stitch — about 6 mm (¼″) along towards you and out again. Continue to repeat this step, allowing some lace to fall into a fold between each stitch. You will probably find it easier to place more pins between the quarter points, as this will help you adjust your lace more easily.

Note: If you find this traditional method of applying lace not to your liking, pull out both ends of the built-in gathering thread found at the straight edge of the lace and gather up the lace to the correct length, then apply it, butting the edge with the seam line and taking tiny stitches to secure it.

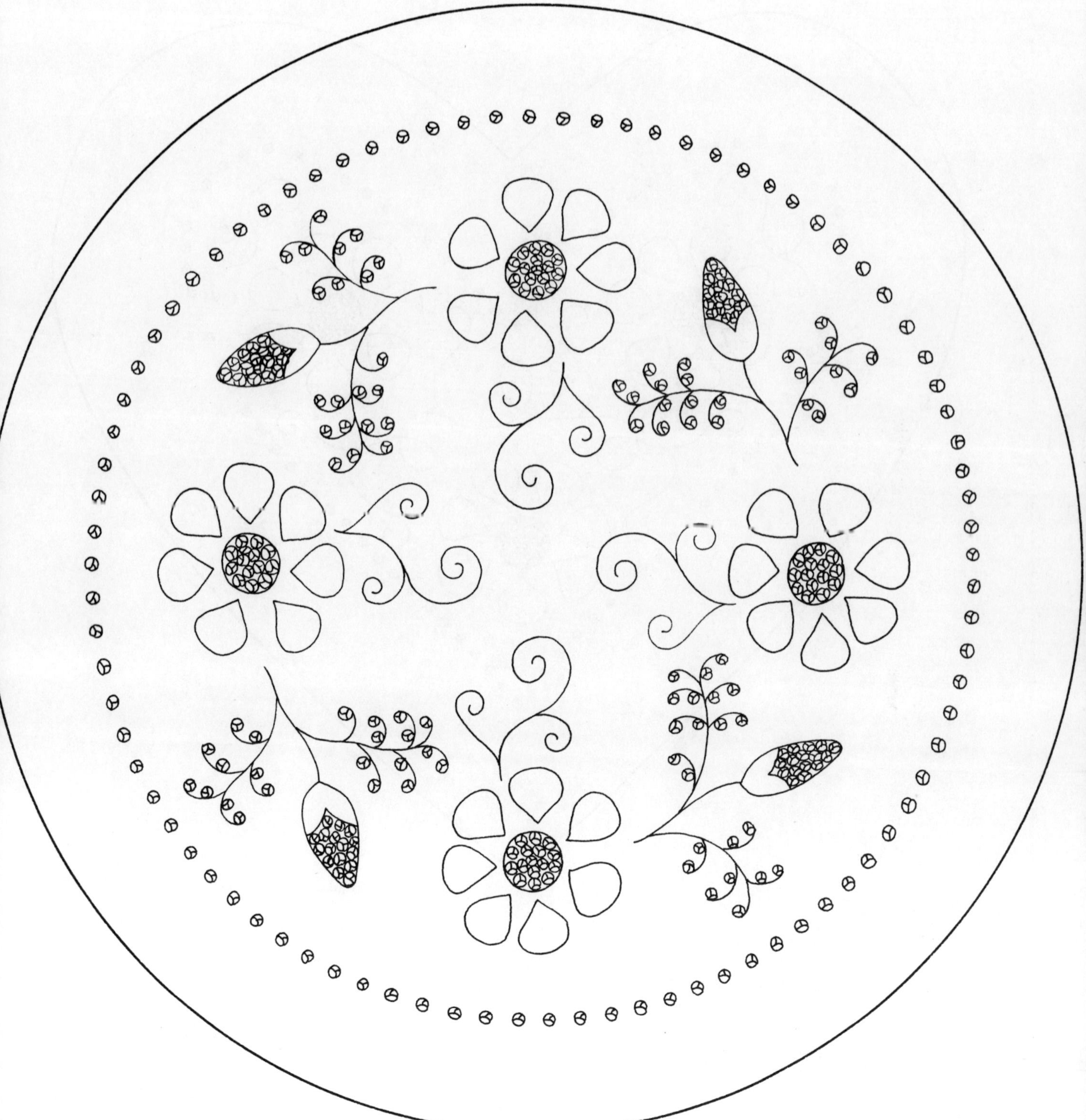

PLATE 2

PLATE 3

PLATE 4

PLATE 5

PLATE 6

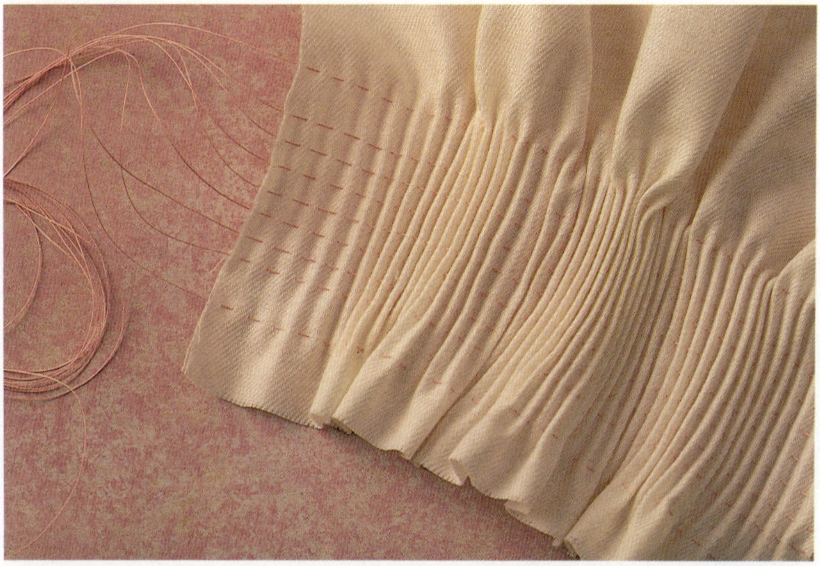

PLATE 7

PLATE 8

Cardboard Carton Doll's House

Take one or two cartons, cover them with fabric after you've cut out doors and windows, line the inner walls, add a roof and — hey presto! — you have a pretty doll's house that will occupy young ladies for hours! There is much of this project that can be changed to suit whatever materials you have to hand, and I don't envisage that you have to spend much money at all to make this doll's house happen. Scraps of fabric, ribbons, small boxes and greeting cards can all be used to decorate your doll's house.

Materials

- *Decide whether you wish a single or double-storey house. Identical cartons stacked together make a two-storey house, using the base of the upper carton as the floor of the second storey*
- *Another carton from which to cut the roof*
- *Fabric to cover inner and outer walls, lace fabric or narrow lace for curtains, felt or velveteen for carpets*
- *Stacks of matchboxes for chests-of-drawers*
- *Pegs for peg dolls*
- *Spray-on glue*
- *A hot-melt gun*
- *Scissors*
- *Masking tape or similar*
- *Sharp craft knife for cutting away the windows and doors*

Method

Tape your boxes together and mark in windows and doors. Cut these out with a craft knife, cutting against a strong ruler, and cut large sections of the back of the doll's house to allow access for play. Decide on a shape for the roof, then cut the extra carton into a roof, taking advantage of one corner angle as the peak of the roof.

Cover all exterior surfaces of house and roof with glued-on fabric, such as calico, turning edges in at windows and doors where possible. Cover all interior walls with fabrics. Run ribbon around to make cornices and skirting rails. Gather lace for pelmets, and let lengths of lace become the curtains.

Glue the roof in place with a glue gun. Add cut-out fabric flowers under the ground floor windows, and as flowers in window boxes at the second level.

Dress a peg in a length of gathered fabric for a skirt, and wrap fabric shawl-like around the upper section for the bodice. Tie a ribbon around the middle. Add small facial features with marker pens.

Stack matchboxes together to create a chest of drawers and tape around the stack to secure them together. Using a glue gun, fasten a loop of ribbon at each 'drawer' to be the pull-handle. Silver paper glued to a wall acts as a mirror. Small paper cut-outs act as pictures on the wall. Small boxes can become beds or cots, with sheets, pillow and cotton-wool mattress. Generally, let your imagination go and make your doll's house as inventive as you wish.

Coiled Place Mats

So often it's the surface of those hard-wearing, cork-backed place mats that gives way first, leaving you reluctant to use the mats at all. Try this easy transformation and your mats will be good for even more years. String or rope of various thicknesses are both suitable. Quantities of rope will depend on the size of your mats and the thickness of the rope or string.

Materials

- *String or rope*
- *PVA glue*
- *Paintbrush*

Method

Starting at the outside edge, paint on a thick layer of glue about 2-3 cm (¾″-1¼″) wide. Push the rope down into the glue and coil it around the mat, keeping the rows butted close together. Just after you start you may be able to conceal the rope's end under the next coil. Continue glueing and coiling until the entire surface is covered with rope. Cut off the rope and tuck the end down well with a little more glue, if necessary. You may wish to give the surface of the rope a coat of 50/50 PVA glue and water mixed together. Simply paint it on and allow to dry. It will not waterproof the surface, but will protect it slightly.

Craft Coiling

This delightfully easy craft is a good example of recycling and can be used to make all kinds of useful things, such as place-mats, pet baskets and needlework baskets. Just let your imagination go. Remember that oval shapes work just as well as round, and that basket sides don't have to be straight — they can be curved gently inwards or outwards.

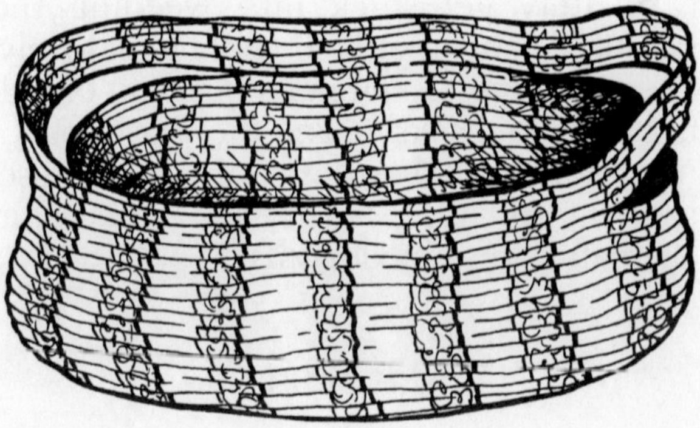

Considerations

You can use pre-used fabrics or scraps cut or torn into 2 cm (1″) wide strips. I prefer to have the strips cut on the bias, but there's nothing wrong with simply ripping the fabric across to create your strips. Some coiling looks effective using different fabrics for a striped effect. Experiment to see what you like best. Estimate the amount of cord you need by coiling a tape measure around to the preferred size; then decide on the depth you need.

Australian-made crushed and twisted paper cord (available from Pioneer Craft, Hornsby, NSW, (02) 477 1239) is a terrific base, and is inexpensive.

Materials

- *Large-eyed tapestry needle; metal is suitable, but you will find the firm, plastic type very much easier to work with*
- *Craft coiling cord. This is available in 6 mm (¼″), 1.2 cm (½″) and 2 cm (1″) diameters. Substitute soft piping cord if this is unavailable*
- *Scissors*
- *Craft glue*

Method

To get started: wind the fabric securely around the end of the cord, then twist the end back over itself by about 1.5 cm (⅝″). Bind these layers together, then wind the cord around a little more and take a stitch over this and back between the first two coils. Continue winding and stitching — you should always be stitching over two rows of coils. Eventually, a pattern will emerge and your stitches will appear to fan outwards from the centre. You may wish to wind the fabric strip around the cord to conceal it in between taking securing stitches. Always pull your fabric strip firmly, and don't worry if the wrong side comes to the surface — it all blends in the end!

Handles must be secure. Be sure to wind extra fabric around the bases of each one. Apply fabric glue to the inside of the basket to help anchor them more securely, especially if a considerable strain is likely to be put on the handle.

Decal-trimmed Garden Tools

This quick 'trim' may not be entirely practical if you are going to immediately get stuck into weeding the petunias — but they'll certainly look lovely! Decals are the contemporary version of old-fashioned transfers — and they have lots of uses. Above all, they are really easy to use, resilient and inexpensive, and provide an alternative to painted motifs.

Materials

- *The object you wish to trim*
- *Decals of your choice (available from craft and decal specialty shops)*

Method

Following the manufacturers instructions, apply the decals to the appropriate area. Flat areas are more suitable, but gentle curves can sometimes be used.

Decorating with String, Rope, Raffia and Shells

It's amazing what you can fashion out of a ball of string, a pile of shells and few lengths of raffia. There's a strong trend towards all things 'natural' in decorating — and it suits our Australian way of life down to the ground. These ideas are inexpensive and require no skill, other than a little patience and some basic skill in arranging objects.

Materials

- *String — jute or natural fibre types are best*
- *Raffia (leftovers from your hat plaiting, or buy a small amount from a craft shop)*
- *Shells — any sort, providing they're not too heavy*
- *Scissors*
- *Hot-melt glue gun*
- *PVA glue (from craft and hardware shops)*
- *Water and a small paintbrush*
- *Whatever you choose to cover or decorate — boxes, trays, place mats and frames, for example*

Method

To wind string or rope around an object, I've found it easier to start from the outside edge and work towards the centre. Don't pull it as you wind — the strands will not sit next to each other — rather allow it to lie where it settles as you wind without any tension being exerted on it. Coat the surface quite thickly with PVA glue first, and keep adding to it as the string or rope soaks it up quickly. Tuck the end in at the very middle after cutting it neatly with scissors. Give the whole surface a coat of glue mixture when completed — blended 50–50 water and glue is good. The string on the sides of boxes should stop just where the lid reaches when it's in position, otherwise the bulk of string will prevent it sitting properly. Cover the top of box lids first, then work down the sides from the top edge.

Shells

Glue them with hot-melt glue to the top of string-covered boxes, and add a bunch of small string tassels to trim.

Very simple tassels

You will need a piece of firm card or board around which you wind your string or raffia. The length of card or board decides the length of tassel you make. Place a 20 cm (8″) (approximately) length of string or raffia across the surface of the winding card. Wind string around the card or board many times — experience will show you how many, depending on the thickness of your material. Clip the end of raffia or string and slide the first horizontal piece of string up and tie it firmly around the top of the loops. Slide the loops off the card or board and wind another piece of string around the loops several times and tie off, making the neck of the tassel. Clip the ends neatly, straight across.

> ### *Tip*
>
> When working with PVA glue your fingers can become sticky — keeping them damp can prevent your fingers accidentally lifting off the recently glued work.

Docile Dinosaurs

These creatures make good pets — they are easy to make and don't eat much! I suggest you stitch their seams on the outside using a machine stitch that resembles buttonhole stitch (or use zig-zag). Or you could sew them completely by hand, using double sewing thread and buttonhole stitch. Dinosaurs like to have names, so please be sure to give your friendly creature a wonderful name!

Materials

- *Felt — take your pattern along when purchasing, as some ready-cut felt squares may be big enough*
- *Polyester fibre stuffing*
- *Small black felt scraps for eyes*
- *Ribbon for neck bow*

Method

You should cut two body shapes, four front and four back legs. Note the pattern showing leg positions and mouth and eye shapes.

1. Placing the legs together in pairs and, starting from the foot, stitch around, leaving a small opening on the 'sole' of the foot for stuffing. Leave long threads on the sewing to use later to hand sew the stuffing opening closed. **Do not join body pieces together at this stage.**
2. Transfer the leg positions to the body pieces by tracing off the markings from the pattern. Place the legs against the body pieces on markings and stitch around from '•' to '•', securing the legs to the body piece through all thicknesses, stitching just in from the edge of the leg.
3. Place the body pieces together (legs outside) with edges matching and stitch around, leaving an opening for stuffing between the legs, along the 'tummy' edge.
4. Stuff the legs first, then the body firmly, hand sewing the openings closed using buttonhole stitch. Cut out two 5 mm-diameter (2″) circles from black felt and glue, or stitch them on as eyes.
5. Stitch in a mouth using dark sewing thread, pulling it slightly through from one side of the face to the other to give some shape.

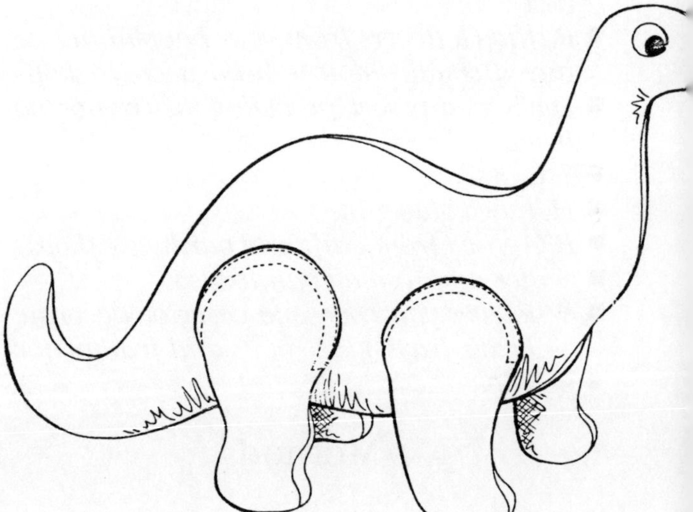

Easy Découpage

Découpage is the gentle art of covering just about any flat surface with paper cut-outs. You can take this easy shortcut by using modern glues and sealers instead of the traditional time-consuming varnish and sanding methods.

Considerations

Découpage can transform many seemingly dull or ordinary items into objects of beauty. Decide on the background colour needed and, if a layer of background paper does not appeal, paint the item first using artists' acrylic paints. Allow to dry well before starting to glue. The composition of motifs needs careful thought. If you have a theme in mind using flowers, animals or faces, for example, you'll need to spend some time searching for the appropriate motifs.

Materials

- *Pieces of wallpaper, wrapping paper, greeting cards, wallpaper borders, magazine clippings — any decorative paper motif which appeals to you*
- *Small, sharp scissors for cutting paper*
- *Objects to be covered — tins, trays, book jackets, papier-mâché figures, picture frames, terracotta pots, coathangers, for example*
- *PVA glue (white, milky glue)*
- *Soft paintbrush*
- *Spray-on lacquer, if desired*

Method

Cut out motifs from paper, either precisely, or leaving a small margin of about 6 mm (¼″) around each one. It is wise to prepare a generous amount of cut-outs prior to starting. This way you can plan your design and not be held up in the gluing process by having to do more searching and cutting out. Plan how you will arrange the motifs on the item to be decorated. Experiment until you reach a pleasing composition. If you intend covering the item completely, you may use a layer of background pieces first. Cut these in random small shapes and overlap them to entirely cover the item. As previously discussed, you may wish to paint the background instead.

If cut-outs are a little stiff to handle (this may be the case if greeting cards have been used), soak them for a few minutes in warm water. Pat dry and use as for the other motifs.

Coat a small area with undiluted glue, place the cut-out motif on the glued area, then coat the motif with glue. Repeat this process until the design is complete. Allow to dry, then coat again with glue. This glue dries to a crystal-clear finish. Apply final coats, as desired, to increase shine. You may decide to finish the item with several light coats of spray-on lacquer.

Easy Director's Chair Cover

There is probably no more adaptable chair today than the director's chair. It's inexpensive, reasonably sturdy and remains stylish regardless of where you place it. Being able to drop different covers over it makes it even more desirable because it can transform a balcony chair into a formal dining room chair at the drop of a cover — and back again in a flash. It can also easily maintain its usefulness throughout the seasons by cover changes with appropriate fabrics. These covers are very simple to make as they have only **two** pattern pieces, and have sufficient ease designed into the pattern to allow for quick fitting and removal of the covers.

Materials

The requirements are for each chair, presuming it is a basic director's chair, with straight arms, back and legs. This pattern does not suit chairs which have backs shaped out at the sides, or those that have only criss-crossed legs and no straight side-support legs. I suggest that you pre-wash your fabric to eliminate shrinkage. Please note that I have allowed only 5 cm (2″) for the hems — you may wish to allow more.

- *3.30 m (11′) of 115 cm-wide (45″-46″) fabric for each cover*
- *Sewing thread*

Method

Draw up your pattern using brown paper or newspaper. Transfer all markings — 1 cm (½″) seams have been included. Read through the instructions first and note the illustrations and stitching sequence — this may make it easier for you. You may like to practise by folding the paper pattern into shape. Once you can see the simplicity of how it's pieced together, you'll be rushing out for more fabric to make more of these covers!

Fold fabric to have right sides facing and cut out two side/arm pieces. Cut one back/front piece with fabric opened up. Bring Bs together on arm pieces and stitch from A to B. Fold C down at Bs and stitch. Match and pin Es through to Fs on back/front piece and side/arm pieces along slight curve and stitch. These curves sit at the back of the seat, where the back and seat meet, and allows for minimum fabric pressure when the cover is in use. Pivot fabric and stitch from Fs through to Cs then down to Gs. Fold fabric to have right sides facing and stitch from Ds through to Es then down side to Hs.

Try cover on chair and turn up hem, press, then stitch.

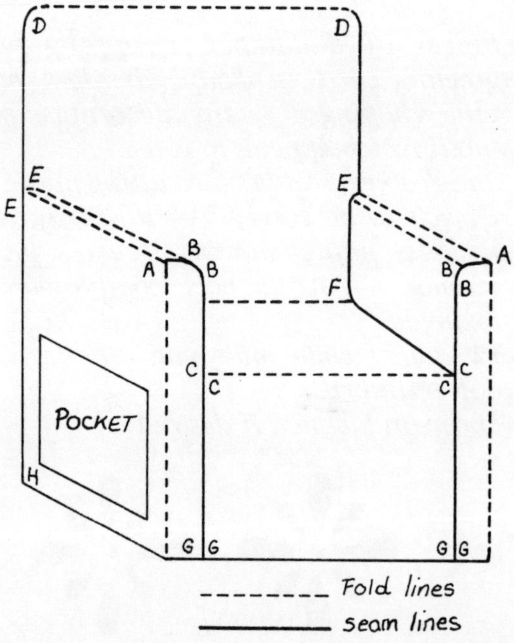

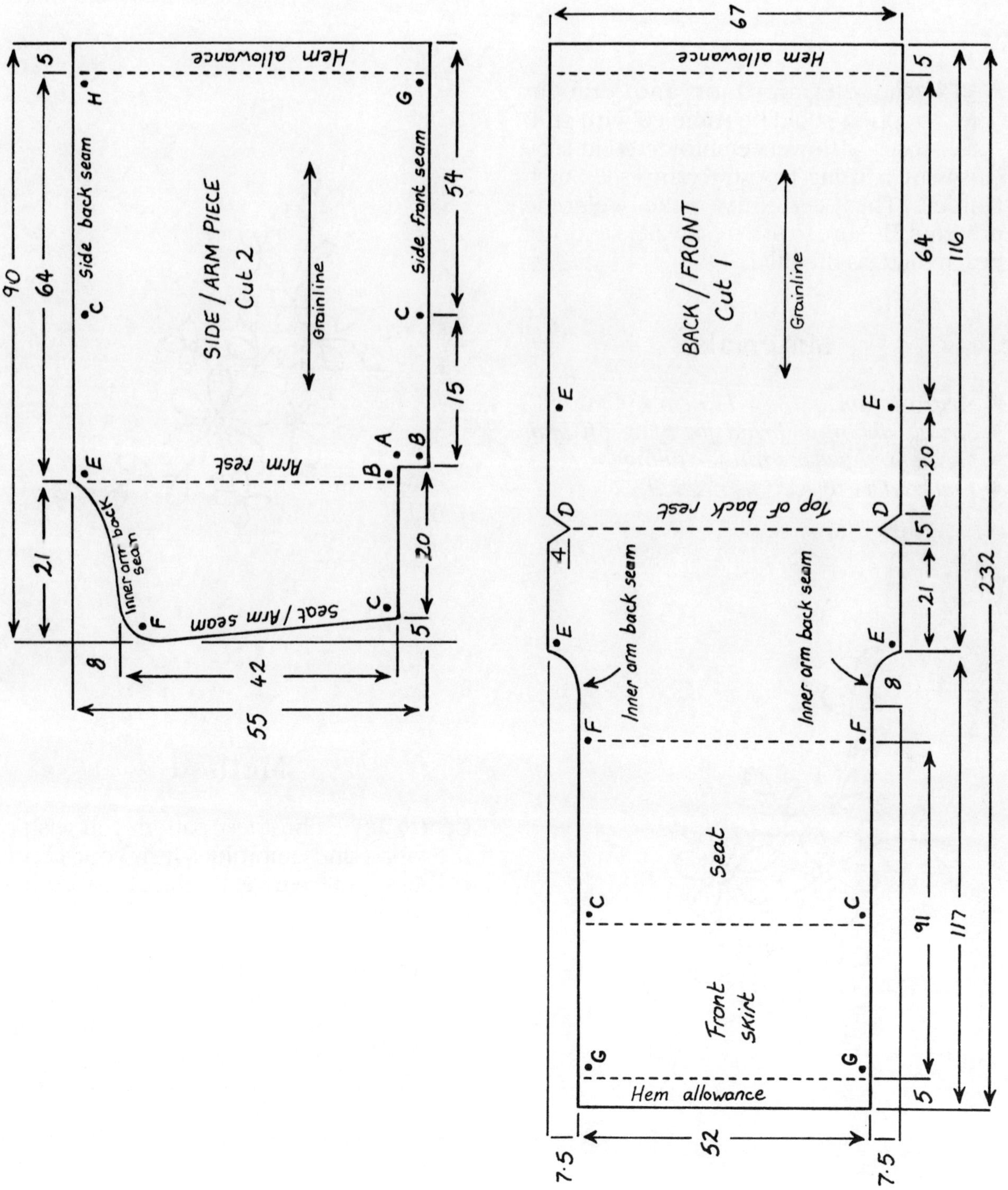
SIDE / ARM PIECE
Cut 2
Grainline
Side back seam
Side front seam
Hem allowance
Arm rest
Inner arm back seam
Seat / Arm seam
BACK / FRONT
Cut 1
Grainline
Hem allowance
Top of back rest
Inner arm back seam
Inner arm back seam
Seat
Front skirt
Hem allowance

Fabric Draught Stoppers

These elegant door and draught stoppers could be trimmed with grub roses or flowers embroidered in lazy-daisy stitch using tapestry yarn (see Stitch Guide). They certainly make welcome presents. Be sure to use freshwater sand, not beach sand, as the filler.

Materials

- *Strip of fabric 23 x 115 cm (9″ x 45″)*
- *Strong ribbon or braid for tying off ends*
- *Clean freshwater sand for filling*
- *Embroidery threads as needed*

Method

Centre any embroidery pattern you wish on the fabric and embroider it in your chosen colours. Alternatively, place embroidery motifs 30 cm (12″) from each end and at the centre.

Fold fabric so that right sides are facing and long edges matching. Stitch long sides in a 1.5 cm (⅝″) seam. Turn in short ends 12 cm (5″) and baste. Turn tube to right side. Tie off one end very securely about 8 cm (3″) from folded end.

Holding open the other end, fill the tube with sand — a funnel will help with this process. When tube is filled to about 9 cm (3½″) from end, tie off open end very securely.

Fairy Wand, Wings and Skirt

There are few little girls who can resist dressing up as a fairy — it's a delightful thing to see a room full of pretty fairies at a birthday party. I'm acquainted with a few small fairies who, once dressed in their fairy finery, strongly resist any parental request to be transformed back into a mere person! Traditional fairy colours are pinks, blues, greens and purples, and are never very bright shades.

Wand

Materials

- *30 cm (11¾″) of 1 cm dowel, or a firm bamboo chopstick*
- *20 cm (8″) square of firm cardboard*
- *PVA glue*
- *Acrylic paints*
- *Glitter, dimensional paints and fake jewels for decoration*
- *Ribbon Roses (optional)*

Method

Cut out a star shape from cardboard. Paint it both sides with acrylic paints. Paint PVA glue thickly onto the centre and over the remainder of the surface. Apply jewels and roses to the centre and sprinkle glitter over the remaining still-wet PVA glue. When glue is dry, draw extra decorations on with squeeze-bottle dimensional paints. Allow the star to dry thoroughly, then apply a thick spread of glue to the back of the star and press the top of the dowel into it. Support it evenly while it's drying. You may add trimmings to the back of the wand too, if desired.

Skirt

Measure your child's length from waist to knee, or as desired, for the length of fabric needed. Tulle is generally available as 150 cm (58″-60″) width fabric.

Materials

- *Skirt length of tulle in each of three different coloured tulles*
- *Waist length of 5 cm-wide (2″) ribbon, plus 10 cm (4″)*
- *Hooks and eyes, buttons or press studs for waist fastening*
- *Scissors and sewing thread*

Method

Fold each piece of tulle evenly into sections and cut one edge into deep zig-zags. Trim away some tulle from the remaining straight edge of two tulle pieces so that the tulle pieces have staggered depths. Place the straight edges together and gather them to the waist measurement, plus 10 cm. Stitch one edge of the ribbon to the back waist gathering of the skirt, folding the remaining edge over and stitching it down over the front waist gathering, folding in the short raw edges of the ribbon to neaten. Apply closures to waist to finish off.

Wings

Materials

- *Two wire coathangers*
- *Pair of pastel-coloured panty-hose or stockings*
- *Dimensional paints*
- *Glitter*
- *PVA glue, or craft paints containing glitter*
- *Elastic for shoulder loops*

Method

Bend the coathangers as shown, clipping off the hook. Cut away the panty section of the pantyhose, leaving two leg pieces. Pull one leg section over each coathanger, having one toe section at the top of each wing, and winding the remainder of the leg section around where the hook was. Pin it in place to secure while you're painting.

Paint the wings using dimensional paints, glue then sprinkle on glitter, or use glitter paints, and you may like to add some silk flowers towards the centre. Paint both sides of the wings, if desired. Allow to dry thoroughly. Overlap the two hook sections and bind with leg ends, stitching them in place by hand. Holding the wings against your child's back, ascertain how long each shoulder loop needs to be. The wings should sit at about the level of the shoulder blades, and the loops should be attached to the connecting bound 'band' so that they can be easily pulled on and off, and yet still hold the wings in place. Hand sew the elastic loops firmly in place once you're satisfied with the fit.

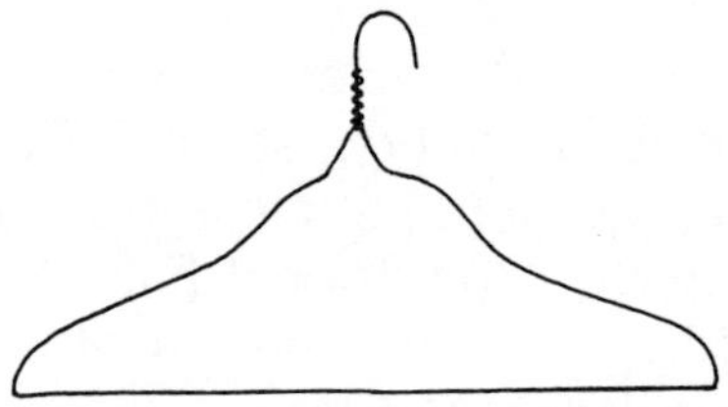

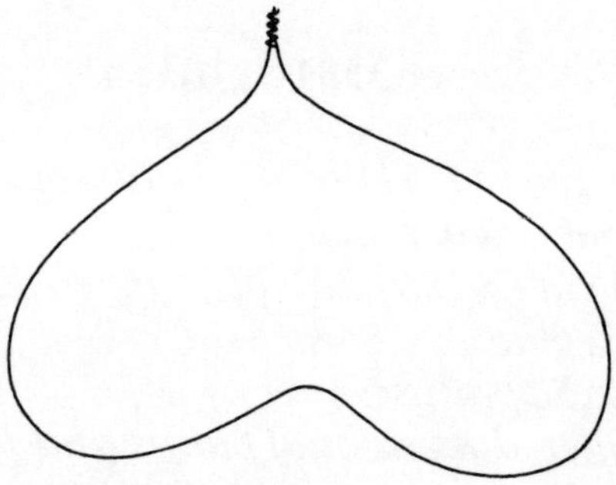

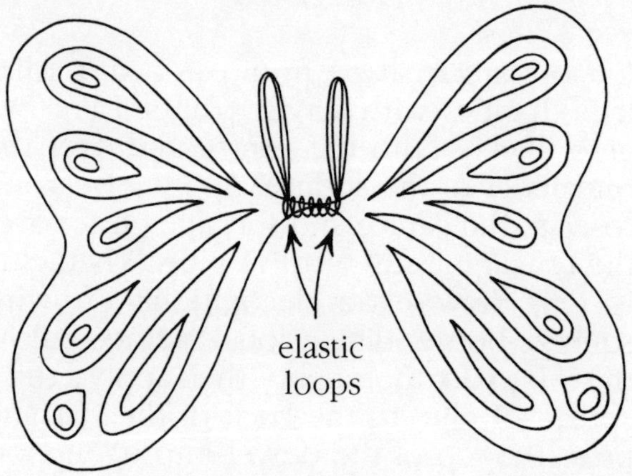

Fireplace Screen

This fireplace screen will provide a decorative focal point for your room all-year round. It is covered with floral fabric or paper cut-outs which are glued into position on a sheet of craft-wood. The shape and size of your fireplace opening will dictate the shape and size of the screen. If, perhaps, you already have a floral fabric or wallpaper in your room, you could consider using motifs from this as cut-outs.

Considerations

Work out an approximate height and width for your screen, based on your fireplace opening and considering the space needed for the basket.

If you cut all your motifs from one style of fabric or paper, you can leave some of the background colour in place. It's almost impossible to cut it all away, in any case. You will need to paint the background of the wood in the same colour so that the fabric background blends in and is not noticeable. If you cut your motifs from several fabrics you will have to cut away all the backgrounds to avoid creating a confusing image. In this case, paint the background a colour of your choice.

Materials

- *A piece of craft-wood or particle board, a little larger than the size of the screen and approximately 1.5 cm (⅝") thick*
- *Fabrics or paper from which you will cut floral motifs*
- *Two angle irons at least 10 x 20 cm (4" x 8") for the supports or legs (note that larger ones may be needed if your screen is very big)*
- *2 cm (1") thick piece of timber at least 23 cm (9") square to act as a support panel to which the angle irons are attached*
- *Screws for the support panel and angle irons*
- *Acrylic paints that tone with floral motifs for painting background, edge of screen and the basket*
- *Power jig-saw or hand-held fret saw*
- *Aquadhere glue or similar product*
- *Small paintbrush for applying glue*
- *Spray-on clear matt or gloss paint*
- *Small, sharp scissors for cutting out fabric motifs*

Method

Paint right side of board with background colour, or other colour of your choice. The back is best painted in a dark colour such as Brunswick green. Cut out flowers carefully from paper or fabric and arrange them on the board to approximate the size of the screen, allowing enough room for the painted basket. Once your arrangement is satisfactory, sketch in a basket and paint, allowing for some flowers to fall over the front of the basket top and soften the edge.

Using the paintbrush, apply glue to the back of the floral motifs and the board, and fix the motifs into position. Paint each motif with another coat of glue once in position. Give the surface another coat of glue once motifs are all in place. When the board is completely dry (this will take about 24 hours) draw around the edge of the motifs, allowing about a 2 cm (1") margin. Check that you have not created any angles that are impossible for the saw to reach. Cut around the flowers and basket using the saw. Smooth off the edges and touch up any background paint chipped away in the sawing process. Paint the edges and back with dark green paint or a similar tone.

Place the screen face down on an old blanket or cloth. Position the support panel at the lower edge of the screen and screw it in place. Screw on the angle irons so that they protrude and support the screen; their base should be 6 mm (¼″) or so up from the edge so that the screen tilts very slightly backwards.

Paint the support panel and angle irons to match the back, touching up paint where needed elsewhere. Seal the entire screen, front and back, with several coats of spray-on clear paint, either in matt or gloss.

Floor Treatments

Staining, stencilling and bleaching wooden floors

Often, the solution to unattractive floors is a modestly priced creative one rather than a bank-breaking hi-tech exercise. These simple solutions with paint, stains and bleach may be the answer for you.

Bleaching

Bleaching will lighten an existing floor colour considerably and can later be sealed with polyurethane paint. Pour bleach on floor and spread with a mop, or similar. Leave until lightness is achieved. The method is particularly suitable for floors that have not been stained, as the stain soaks into the fibres of the timber and is difficult to eliminate completely. However, bleaching can lighten an existing stain to a certain degree. If the timber has been treated with stain and a polyurethane sealer in the past, it must first be sanded back to the stained timber. Ensure that you have good ventilation while you're working with bleach as the fumes it gives off can be irritating.

Neutralise your bleached floor with a solution of five parts water to one part white vinegar once you are satisfied with the degree of bleaching achieved. Be patient with this process — it does take a while to achieve a proper, bleached look, and you should not anticipate using the room for a while. To finish, seal the dry floor with polyurethane paint.

Liming

This method simply involves an application of a watered-down acrylic paint, or an oil-based paint that has been thinned substantially with turpentine or paint thinners. This mixture is painted onto the unstained floor and left on the wood for a very short time only. You then wipe off the excess paint with a lint-free cloth, following the wood grain. A light-coloured tone is the result. Keep applying paint until you achieve the strength of colour you desire. To finish, seal the dry floor with polyurethane paint.

Stencilling

Stencilled floors have certainly stood the test of time. Creative people have long painted their floors, not only to save money, but to bring an individual touch to their home's atmosphere. Floors are transformed from being merely a platform to fulfilling a strong, decorative role in a room.

Stencilling can be done on a previously stained and sealed floor, although you will have to lightly sand the top surface in order for the stencil paint to adhere.

Borders work well on floors, especially as a frame for rugs or to edge a hallway. They can be used to define certain areas of a large room; for example, to divide a lounge area from a dining area. Use a commercial stencil, or cut your own design that perhaps reflects some decorative motif already in your room. Use acrylic paints, and be sure to sand the floor lightly prior to painting so that the paint adheres to the floor. To finish, seal the stencil and floor when dry with polyurethane sealer.

Painting

A floor that has been well worn is sometimes beyond stripping and staining. Odd floor boards, badly nailed boards or even gaps can make staining unviable. Painting can be a good solution in these instances. Patch up nail holes or gaps first, using a proprietary filler. Use several coats of heavy-duty acrylic or oil paint, allowing each coat to dry thoroughly before you apply more. Perhaps you could stencil over the paint. Remember to start painting at the furthest corner to the door, working your way back across the room to the doorway. You'll be in trouble if you don't!

Frilled Cushion Covers

Making these covers is simple — you can insert matching piping between the frill and the cushion front if you like — and the two-coloured frill is a trick I discovered years ago that will give your cushions a terrific decorator touch with minimum effort from you! Remember that cushions and lamps are the single most effective items when it comes to giving a room a low-cost make-over. The quantities given apply to one 40 cm (16″) square cushion, which fits the most common cushion insert available. Vary your materials according to your own choice of size.

Materials

- *1 fabric piece, 42 cm (16½″) square for cushion front*
- *2 fabric pieces, 42 cm x 23 cm (16½″ x 9″) for cushion back*
- *Strips of 8 cm-wide (3¼″) fabric for frill, totalling 3.20 m (4 yd) in length*
  Strips of 10 cm wide (4″) fabric (for narrow feature edge and frill back) totalling 3.20 m (4 yd) in length
- *1 x 35 cm (14″) zipper*
- *Optional ready-made or matching fabric piping*
  One 40 cm (16″) square polyester fibre cushion insert (or similar)

Method

Prepare the frill by first joining the short ends of the strips of each fabric into two circles. Place together one long edge of each circle, right sides facing, and stitch, taking a 1 cm (½″) seam. Press the seam to one side as you press the pieces flat. Fold the fabrics to have their remaining edge matching and press. This will give you a border and frill back of one fabric with the other fabric making up the widest front part of the frill. Divide the frill into four equal parts and take a small notch at these marks in the seam allowance. Gather between these notches with a double row of gathering stitching.

Join together the two back pieces along the 42 cm (16½″) edges taking a 2 cm (16½″) wide seam, leaving a 35 cm (14″) gap (or however long your zipper is) and press open the seam. Insert zipper, leaving zipper open.

Using a sewing machine zipper foot, stitch optional piping around cushion front, with right sides facing and matching raw edges. Place the frill against the cushion front, right sides facing and raw edges matching, then pin. To attach frill, stitch between rows of gathering, then remove gathers. Push frill towards cushion centre and place back over front, right sides facing and raw edges matching. Stitch around, just inside frill stitching. Turn cushion cover to right side, and place cushion insert inside.

Garden or Tool Apron

Make one of these for your favourite family handyman or gardener. They are simple yet very practical garments and can be made from sturdy, plain-coloured scrap fabric.

Materials

- *50 cm (20") of sturdy fabric 115 cm (45") wide*
- *Sewing thread*

Cutting notes

Cut three rectangular shapes approximately 40 x 27 cm (16″ x 10½″) and one that is 40 x 32 cm (16″ x 13″). Cut a long strip for the waistband that is 10 cm (4″) wide.

Method

Place two of the smaller rectangles together, and round off the two lower corners using a glass tumbler as a guide. Fold over the 40 x 32 cm (16″ x 13″) rectangle widthways and press in half. Round off the two unfolded corners to match the other rounded corners.

Place folded piece onto large pieces, matching round corners, and baste to secure. Place the third smaller rectangle over basted pieces, with right sides facing, and stitch around sides and base, through all thicknesses. Trim away excess fabric and clip corners for ease. Turn apron to right side and press neatly. Edge stitch around edge 1 cm (½″) from seam. Stitch at intervals through pocket, dividing it into sections for tools, seeds or nails.

Stitch waistband to top of apron, taking a 'tuck' in the tool apron band just to the side of the apron. This should be big enough for the handle of a hammer to slide through.

Garland Country-style

A floral garland is easy to make, and can be a true decorator item. To help you understand the process of trimming your garland, I suggest you read through the instructions before you start. The suggested trimmings will produce a very country-style garland, though you could vary these to suit your own style. The method of inserting the trimmings and holding them in place is suitable for any lightweight trimming.

Materials

- *Garland base of handwoven pussy willow, or similar*
- *Small piece of ribbon for hanging garland*
- *Thick PVA glue, or hot-melt glue gun*
- *Approximately 7 bunches of waxed fruit*
- *Approximately 16 silk roses (about 2 bunches)*
- *Wheat, either bearded or smooth, or some other grain*
- *Sprigs of coloured flowers*
- *Dried reindeer, or sphagnum moss, for filling in the gaps*
- *Scissors or secateurs for cutting thin twigs and other trimmings*

Method

Set up a work place that can be protected by an old towel, sheet of plastic, or similar. If using PVA glue, pour a little into a container such as an egg cup, or similar, and cover it with plastic wrap to prevent it drying out.

The key to making a garland is to insert the trimmings *all in one direction*, that is, all the heads of the trimming end up facing in one direction. You will find that right-handed people may instinctively work clockwise, left-handed people may want to work anti-clockwise. When you have trimmed your garland and arrived back at the starting point, gently lift the heads of the first trimmings you fastened and tuck the last few stems in underneath them. You should not be able to see your start/finish point after this.

Gently spread apart the wired fruit and leaves of the waxed fruit bunches and then insert them into the front of the base, spacing them evenly around it and alternating the colours, if needed. To insert them is simply a matter of tucking the stems into a cavity in the strands of the base. Once you are satisfied with the positions, remove them one by one and dip the stem into the glue, wiping away all excess before tucking the stem back into position in the base. If using hot-melt glue, leave the trimming in place and squeeze hot glue over the stem, securing it in place.

There are two methods of arranging the remaining trimmings. You may choose to space the roses and native flower sprigs evenly, then return and insert the wheat. Or, you may choose to insert all these at random around the base. The choice is yours, but I would suggest that a beginner may be better choosing the first method. You should not worry that your garland will look too methodical or symetrical if you place your trimmings in sequence, as the wheat will be of different sizes and the moss will be placed at random, anyway.

You will probably need to shorten the rose stems to about 5–6 cm (2″-2½″), trim the stems of the flower sprigs individually, and cut the wheat stems to about 8 cm (3½″)

in length. Continue inserting and glueing the remaining trimmings using your chosen method. The wheat will give the garland a look of fullness and you should position each wheat stem so that it faces up and away from the base, rather than have it lying along the base. You will be able to bend the rose heads to any direction you desire, and re-shape the waxed fruit and leaves into more pleasing positions if you find either becoming too concealed by the wheat.

Be sure to cover the outer and inner edges of the base (but not the back) with trimmings. When the garland hangs it can look very bare in profile if the edges are not trimmed.

When all the main trimmings are in place, place small streaks of glue onto any bare areas and push down teased-out small bundles of moss onto this glue. You may wish to experiment with the amount of moss before you use the glue. When glueing is complete, hold up the garland and decide where the 'top' should be. Thread the ribbon through strands of the base at the back and tie the ribbon ends together. Try not to have the ribbon showing if the garland is hanging.

Greeting Cards

The cost of pretty cards can sometimes equal the cost of the present! Here are some ideas for making personalised cards. Most cards are cut from basic, coloured (or painted), firm cardboard.

Creative suggestions

- *Take a bunch of small artificial flowers apart and glue them onto a card to create a posy — position the stems in the direction of the 'tie' around the posy. Attach a small 3 mm (1/8") wide satin ribbon bow at the intersection of the stems.*
- *Cut out large letters — the recipient's initials — and use these as a card. Join them together with ribbons, or if space on the cardboard permits, join them together as you draw them, prior to cutting.*
- *Use a well-dried gum leaf and write your message with felt-tipped pen. This is a good one for men's presents, and looks particularly good if the present is wrapped in brown paper and tied with interesting twine. Tuck a few gum nuts under the bow.*
- *Write your message with liquid glue — then quickly cover the still-wet glue with confetti — or glitter. Dust off excess, and allow card to dry competely before folding.*
- *Simply attach a small dried flower — or a bow — to the corner of unprinted business cards. These are always handy to have close by, and are lifesavers for that overlooked celebration!*
- *Use biscuit-cutter shapes to trace around for interesting cards. Punch a hole using a paper hole-punch and thread a loop of metallic sewing thread or narrow ribbon through for hanging or attaching to the present.*
- *Purchase colourful stickers from your newsagent and use them on plain cards as above, or on cut-out shapes from coloured cardboard. These are fairly expensive, but very quick and effective, and still cheaper than purchased cards.*
- *Stencil your own Christmas cards. Make a Christmas motif stencil and produce your own original cards in quantities to suit. Purchase gold and silver acrylic paint and add some glitter — the children will love making these.*

Ideas on How to Decorate Hats

There are plenty of inexpensive plain straw hats around that are flatteringly shaped, and that are crying out for decoration. The ideas below will give you some ideas on trimming options that will have your hat quickly looking like a million dollars!

Method

- *Hire a top hat or a bowler. Tie a 3 m (3¾") length of black or coloured hat veiling around the crown into a large bow at the back. Add artificial flowers around the crown, or add an extra length of black lace, also tied at the back. You may like to tie knots in the lace at even intervals before fastening it at the back, under the veiling bow.*
- *Purchase approximately 20 bunches of small fabric flowers from your craft supplier. Lay one bunch over the stems of another and fasten them together by binding the stems together with fine fuse wire. Add another bunch and repeat the process, continuing to do this until the length of bunches will wrap around the crown of your hat. Fasten the stems of the last bunch under the flowers of the first bunch to create a wreath-shape. Drop this over the crown of your hat and take a few stitches through the straw to fasten it in place. When the Cup is over, use the wreath of flowers as a wall decoration!*
- *This trimming method involves plaiting, and ideally, the panel of plaiting should sit in the middle of the lengths of veiling, so that the loose ends can be tied into a bow. A little trial and error may be needed to find just where you should start plaiting. Plait together three different colours of 3 m (3¾ yd) lengths of hat veiling until the plaiting is equal to the circumference of your hat crown. Tie the ends at the back of the hat in a big bow, allowing the tails to drop down the back of the hat. Paint on a stripe of one veiling colour around the edge of the hat brim, using artist's acrylic paints.*
- *Drape the hat crown with tulle, stitching it to hold it in place. Using the same soft fabric as your blouse, take a length of fabric around over the tulle, tucking in the raw edges, and taking stitches to form it into gentle folds. The tulle will help build up the depth of the fabric, making it appear more luxurious. If you were to drape the hat totally with the fabric, the result may be too heavy.*
- *Copy the* Pretty Woman *hat by tying a band of polka-dot fabric around the crown and into a large, floppy bow at the back. Make a fabric flower in the following way: cut a length of bias fabric 45-50 cm (18"-20") long x 10-12 cm (4"-5") wide. Fold it over so that long raw edges meet and right side is outwards. Gather along the raw edges. Draw up the gathers slightly. Fold down a short raw end to meet the gathering stitch and commence to roll the fabric around, keeping the gathered edges even. Take occasional pleats in the gathered edge to add to the flower shape. Stitch by hand to hold the roll, continuing to roll and stitch until a flower shape has been made. Take the remaining raw short end down to the base and stitch it to secure. Fasten this flower over the knot of the bow with hand stitches.*

Inexpensive, Practical and Quick-to-make Christmas Presents and Decorations

Painted boxes

These papier mâché boxes can be bought inexpensively from craft shops in sets, or singly. Paint them with acrylic paints then stencil a Christmas motif onto them. Fill them with biscuits or sweets.

Plastic Bag dispenser

Fold a fabric piece 40 cm x 90 cm (16″ x 1 yd) in half lengthways and stitch the long raw edges together, leaving a gap 5 cm (2″) down from the top that measures 20 cms (8″). Stitch back the seam allowance around the gap. Fold over the lower edge and stitch a casing, then thread elastic through the casing, leaving the opening about the size of a small apple. Make a casing at the top edge too, then thread strong cord through it and draw the opening closed. Knot the ends of the cord together and use this for hanging. Add a fabric bow at the top of the front opening, if desired. Place plastic bags into the dispenser one by one, pushing them down into the cavity. Bags can be removed one at a time from the lower opening.

Painted Candles

Using a gold or silver 'paint pen', draw stars over the surface of plain candles. Fill in gaps with small groups of three dots. Allow the 'paint' to dry well before wrapping the candles in pairs with pretty tartan, gold or silver ribbon, or raffia. These pens are available from newsagencies.

Busy Apron

Cut a child-sized classic 'butcher's apron' shape from strong fabric and stitch an assortment of pockets to the front and 'skirt'. Bind the edges with bias binding or turn in hems, and add adjustable straps that button into a buttonhole at the waist of the apron. Fill the pockets with treasures such as pens, pencils, sticky tape, stickers and blunt paper scissors.

Trimmed Bears

Purchase bears from a craft shop and trim them by gathering a length of good quality crocheted lace around their necks and adding a checked ribbon bow. Most crocheted laces have a built-in gathering thread and it's easy to simply draw this thread up from both ends of the lace, tying them in a bow at the back to secure. Adjust the gathers, then hand sew or glue the ends to overlap.

Pine Cone Pin Cushion

Cut the stem end off a well-formed pine cone so that it sits on a flat base. Make small bundles of fabric by cutting squares from a pretty print fabric and bundling them 'pudding fashion' around cotton wool balls and tying with thread to secure. Push these into the openings in the cone, having coated inside the openings with PVA or similar craft glue. Glue small ribbon bows to top.

Interfacing

There are often decisions to make about using interfacing in sewing — and, confusingly, there are often several products from which to choose. The following pointers may help you.

A large variety of interfacing is available, and usually only black or white as far as the home sewer is concerned. There are woven types — similar to woven fabric — as well as non-woven ones which resemble a sheet of flexible paper. Most are synthetic, although some woven interfacings have a cotton content. Iron-on interfacings have one surface coated with glue; this melts when heat us applied, bonding the interfacing permanently to the fabric.

Weights

Various weights of interfacing are available. The lightweights are necessary for light fabrics, while the heavier types are used in belts or tailoring. If in doubt about which weight to choose, lean towards the lighter one. Nothing makes a garment look more 'homemade' than collars, cuffs and facings that are too stiff, bulky or awkward. The purpose of interfacing is to give light support to these areas, not to make them super-stiff.

Iron-on

Be careful when applying iron-on interfacing. While it is certainly a tremendous aid to home sewers, there are several considerations to be made before applying it. Quite a high heat is required to make it bond properly, and this heat can be too high for some synthetic fabrics to endure without damage. If you wish to use iron-on interfacing, I suggest you place a pressing cloth between the iron and the fabric to prevent scorching. Pressure is important in bonding iron-on interfacing, so be sure to press heavily onto the fabric with the iron.

Iron-on interfacing will make the fabric quite stiff. As this effect may be quite wrong with a soft, supple fabric, a lightweight sew-in interfacing — preferably a woven one — may be best here.

Other Fabrics

Sometimes a lightweight fabric, such as preshrunk lawn or organza, can be excellent as an interfacing. Fabrics of this kind provide a firmness without stiffness. Use in areas where you would normally put interfacing. Sometimes simply using a layer of the main fabric as interfacing can be suitable; that is, providing it is lightweight and plain coloured. Silks are a good example here. Another layer of fine silk may be all that is needed to keep collars and facings in place.

Woven interfacings are ideal for tailoring. They have the give needed over shaped areas, and are traditionally used in several weights, from very light to canvas-weight, in men's tailoring.

Stretch iron-on interfacing is now available for using with stretch fabrics. It is applied in the same way as other iron-on interfacings, and is made with small splits which give with the stretch of the fabric.

PLATE 9

PLATE 10

PLATE 11

PLATE 12

Jigsaw Blocks

According to the *Guinness Book of Records*, the earliest known jigsaws were made from 'dissected maps' by John Spilsbury in Drury Lane, London, in about 1762. The world's biggest jigsaw puzzle is about 10 000 square feet in size and again was made in England, in 1990. That is about the size of an average block of land!

It's easy to make simple puzzles for children to use. A proper tool for making puzzles is a jig saw — an old-fashioned tool that allowed you to cut in and around intricate curves and corners. Today, this tool is mechanised and if you have one you are in an ideal position to make your own puzzles most professionally. A fret saw is a similar hand tool, and is readily available at your hardware store.

Glue maps, pictures, calendar scenes, photographs, children's drawings, nursery paintings, wallpaper, greeting cards, and other similar pictures, to wood, using wood glue, or spray adhesive especially for paper. Thin craft wood is good, old bread boards, foam board (thick cardboard sandwiching a layer of foam), thick cardboard or, if all else fails, a sheet of cardboard from a carton. A 'temporary' puzzle can be made quickly from any cardboard or thick paper, really. You can even cut up pictures from unwanted magazines and ask children to re-assemble them.

It will be difficult to cut curves in this cardboard, but you can cut angles and odd shapes. When sticking pictures to children's blocks, use a PVA glue which will stick to the wood block well. You can easily make your own blocks to cover by cutting up a length of timber, such as pine, into geometric shapes, then sanding the edges and sides to be smooth. You may choose to hold the blocks together and glue the complete picture over the surface of the blocks, later splitting them apart with a sharp blade. Or you may cut individual pieces and apply each of them to the surface of the block.

When you have a puzzle of squares, you have no shapes that will 'lock' together, so you may have to confine the puzzle in a frame of some sort to stop it moving unexpectedly.

Kids' Crafts

There are many instructive activities that can keep children thoughtfully occupied. These involve household equipment, paint, play-dough and lots of water — all inexpensive. The ideas given here are for children of around kindergarten age. I must thank Jenny Mackenzie and her excellent book *Fun Crafts for Kids* (JB Fairfax Press) for some of my sources of inspiration. You will undoubtedly need inexpensive non-toxic glue for many children's activities — the recipe below is a good, reliable one.

Boiled Flour Glue

Ingredients and method

Mix together 60 g (½ cup) plain flour and ¾ cup (180 ml) cold water in a saucepan until it becomes a smooth paste. Bring to the boil over a low heat, stirring constantly, until it becomes quite thick. You can add more cold water to thin the paste. Add 1 tablespoon of household disinfectant if you wish to keep the glue. Store glue in a screw-top jar in the refrigerator when not in use.

Uncooked Play Dough

Materials

- *4 cups of plain flour*
- *2 cups cooking salt*
- *Vegetable colouring (optional)*
- *2 cups tepid water, contained in a jug*

Method

Mix all the dry ingredients in a large mixing bowl using a wooden spoon, then add the oil. If you are using vegetable colouring to tint your dough, add it to the water and stir in well.

Pour the water into the dry ingredients, only a little at a time, stirring well as you pour. As the mixture takes up the water, discard the spoon and start kneading the dough. Add more flour if the dough appears to be a little sticky.

When it is formed into a well-kneaded, firm mass transfer it to a floured plastic bag and store it in the refrigerator until it's required. Store dough in the refrigerator between uses.

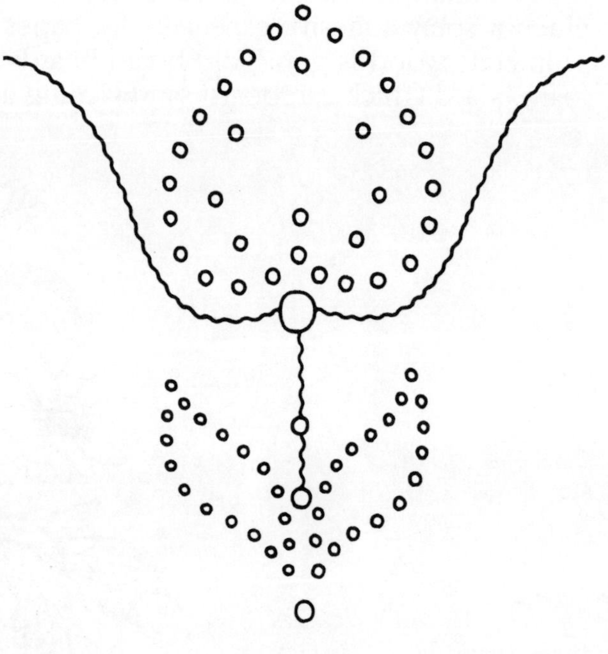

Simple craft ideas

- *Make simple glove puppets from felt and let the child draw the facial features with fabric pens. Or, draw a small face on the palm side of each of the child's fingers and thumbs to make 10 small puppets.*
- *Sewing can be just as much a means of making illustrations as painting. Thread a large tapestry needle with knitting yarn and let the child 'draw' by stitching the yarn onto a piece of clean hessian. You will have to emphasise that the needle must not be pulled tightly or the cloth will pucker.*
- *Make paper jewellery from magazine scraps. Cut 4 x 3 x 3 cm (1⅝" x 1¼" x 1¼") triangles from paper. Put a strip of glue down the middle of the triangle, ending at the 3 cm (1¼") point. Roll the triangles around a pencil, or knitting needle, starting at the widest side of each triangle. Place more craft glue under the point if necessary and press the roll together firmly. Allow the rolls to dry, then string them together to make a necklace.*
- *Make handprints by letting the child dip his or her hands in non-toxic paint and then pressing them onto paper. Cut away most of the background paper and hang these prints on a mobile. Footprints can be fun, too, but take care no one slips over.*
- *Put a puddle of fairly watery paint on a large sheet of paper. Children can then blow through a straw to move the paint around. Or, place large, flat blobs of paint onto the paper, fold the paper over evenly and press. The results are mirrored on both sides and can look quite magical.*
- *Cut shapes on one side of a potato — triangles and stars are good — and use these to make prints on paper. Place paint in a shallow container and dip the shape into it. Then press it firmly onto paper to leave the design.*
- *Make a collage of all sorts of scraps — fabric, cup-cake holders, confetti, milk-bottle tops, twigs, leaves, shells, yarn, paper or feathers are all good — by gluing them at random onto firm paper.*

Lined Picnic Basket

Pictures tell a thousand words, so they say, so here are some step-by-step illustrations showing you how to line a conventional oblong-shaped cane picnic basket, with a handle. The lining itself is lined, and is a simple lift-out design kept in place by fabric strips tied into bows. Perhaps you could add to the effect by making a tablecloth and matching napkins. The size of your basket will dictate the amount of fabric required, but around 1 m (1¼ yd) each of lining and main fabric should be sufficient. Take your pattern with you, when purchasing fabric, to remove any doubts.

1. Place paper pieces inside the basket against the inner sides and base and press your thumbnail in to mark out the shapes of the base and sides. Note, at this stage, how much overhang you wish your basket lining to have, that is, how much it should come over the rim of the basket and down the outside. Mark in space for handle base in long sides.

2, 3, 4. Cut out each section — a base, handle sides, short sides. Your pattern pieces should look something like this. Add 1 cm (½″) all round for seams.

5. Cut one base, two handle sides and two short sides from main fabric, and duplicate this from lining fabric. Join the seams as shown, making a circle each from main fabric and lining fabric. Place lining and main bases together, edges matching and wrong sides facing, and pin around the edges, then overcast.
6. Place main and lining circles together, right sides facing and raw edges matching. Stitch as shown, clipping 'V's from the handle holes for ease. Turn to right side and press seamed edge neatly. Overcast remaining raw edges together. Attach base, matching corners of base to corners of joined sides.
7. Make four 35 cm-long (14″) fabric strips from scrap fabric. Insert the lining into the basket and adjust the overhang. Pin on the strips to the outside, either side of the handle, so that they will tie easily into place. Stitch on the ends of the bow strips securely.

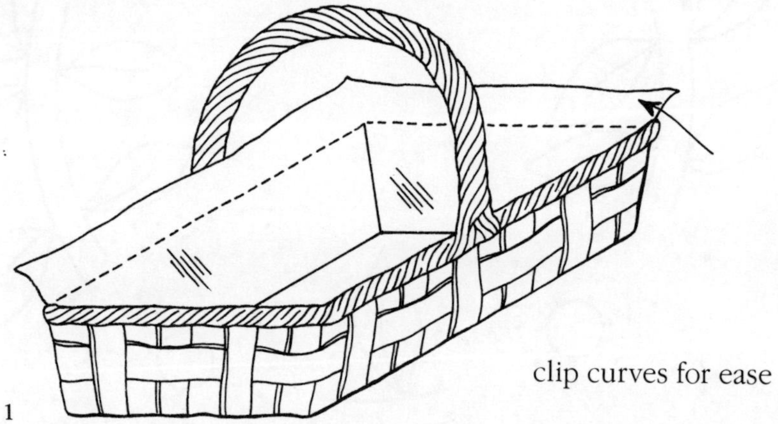

1

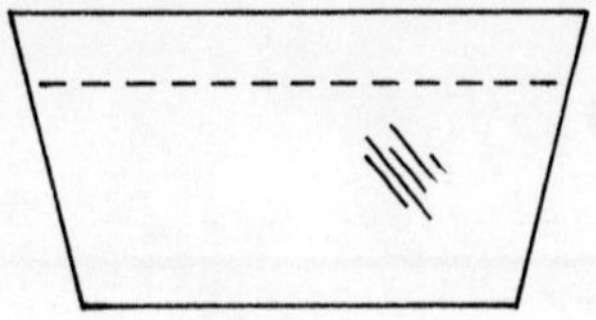

2

ENDS

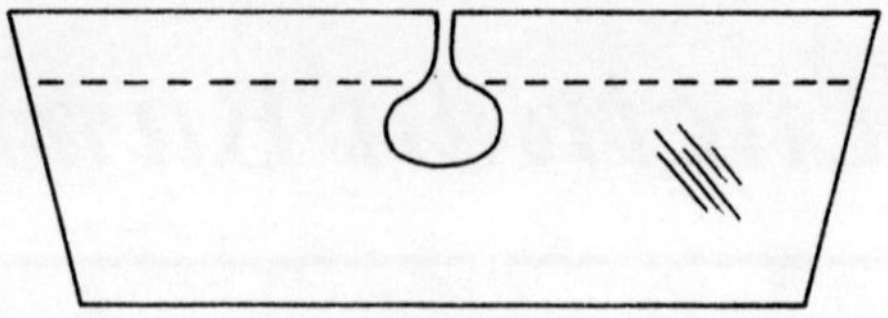

3

SIDES

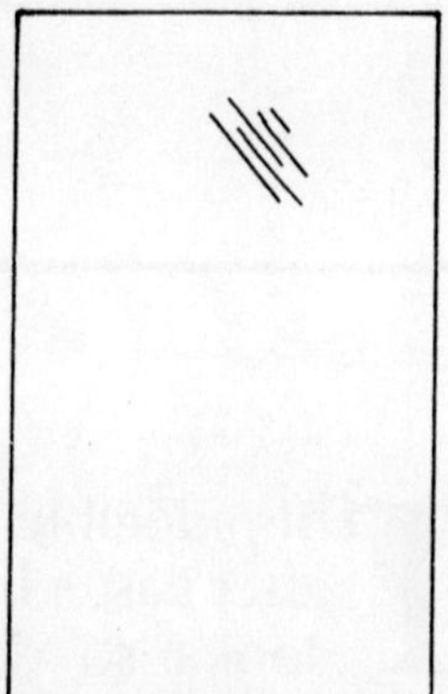

4

BASE

stitching line

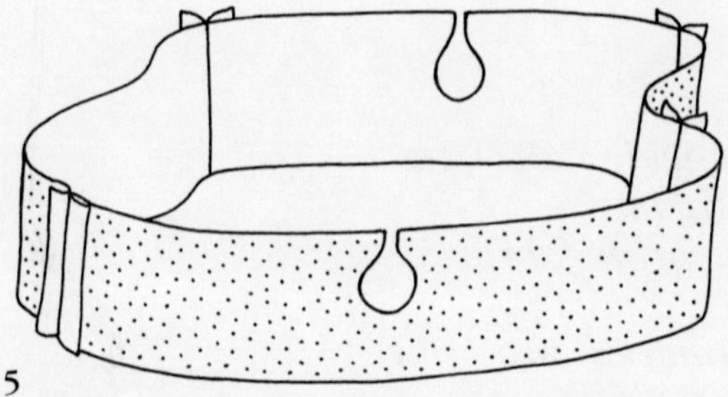

5

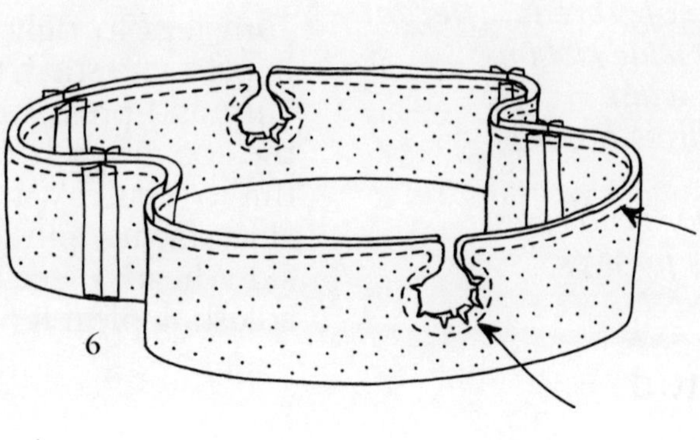

6

7

Lucinda Bunny

This adorable rabbit will be loved long after Easter has come and gone — she looks so demure in her rosebud-trimmed ears and pretty dress and pantaloons, I'm sure you won't be able to resist making her.

Materials

- *1 m (1¼ yd) of 120 cm-wide (48") cotton muslin or calico for rabbit*
- *120 cm (48") of cotton print fabric for dress and pantaloons*
- *4 m (5 yd) of pre-gathered lace for trimming*
- *1 m x 1.5 cm-wide (1¼ yd x ⅝") ribbon for waist trim*
- *2 m (2½ yd) each of three different coloured 3 mm (⅛") wide ribbons*
- *Elastic for pantaloon waist*
- *Press studs for back dress closure*
- *Stuffing for rabbit*
- *Embroidery threads for grub roses*
- *Safety eyes or buttons for eyes*

Method

See pattern pieces on pattern sheet at back of book. Cut out four ears, two side heads, one head centre, two bodies, four arms, four legs for rabbit. Cut out two sleeves, one dress skirt, two front bodices, four back bodices, two front/back pantaloon pieces for dress and pantaloons.

To make Rabbit

(References to illustrations are shown in brackets)
Place legs in pairs and stitch around curved edges, leaving top openings unstitched and an opening at centre back for stuffing (1).

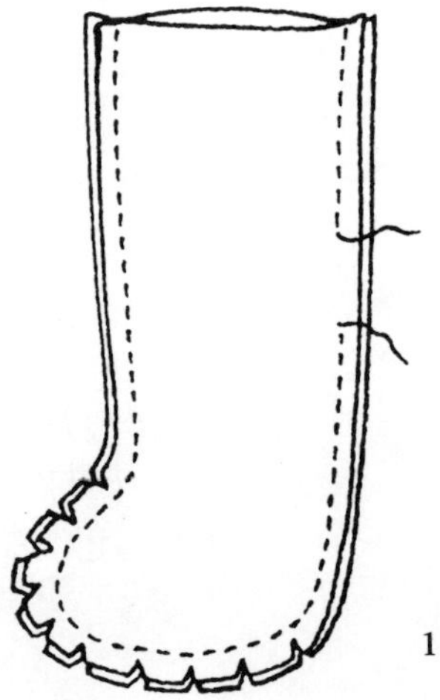

1

Turn legs to right side. Place ears together in pairs and stitch together on curved edges. Turn and press well. Make a small pleat in the top of each ear at raw edges and pin this to secure. With raw edges even and right sides facing, pin an ear to the top of each side head piece between ear markings, adjusting pleat if necessary.

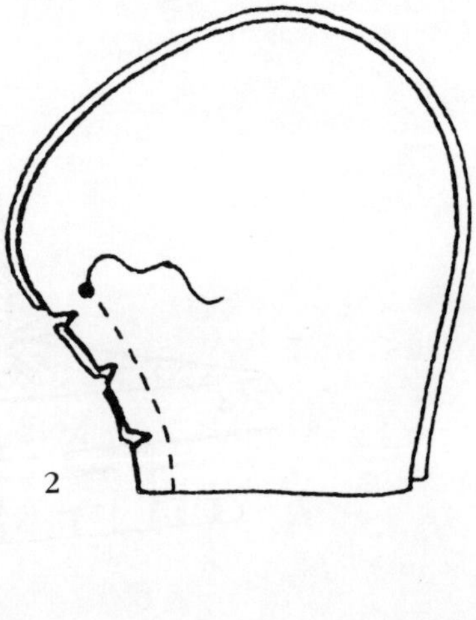

2

Place side head pieces together and stitch from front neck edge to nose position large dot (2). Stay stitch the head centre piece and nick the edges for ease (3). Stitch the head centre piece to side head pieces, stitching from back neck and finishing on each side at large dot. You may have to ease this piece in (4). These seams will also attach the ears (5). Turn head to right side.

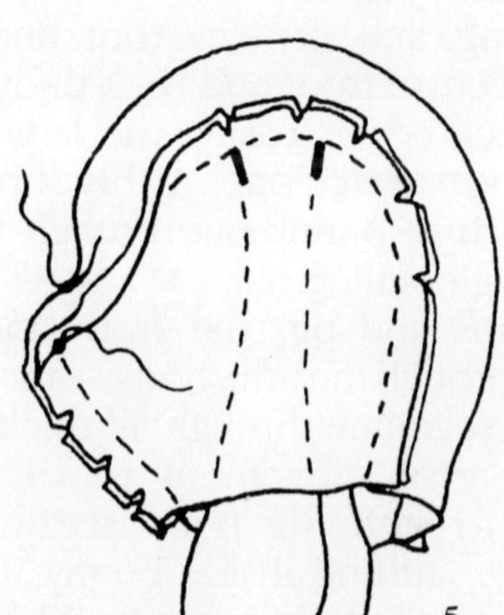

5

3

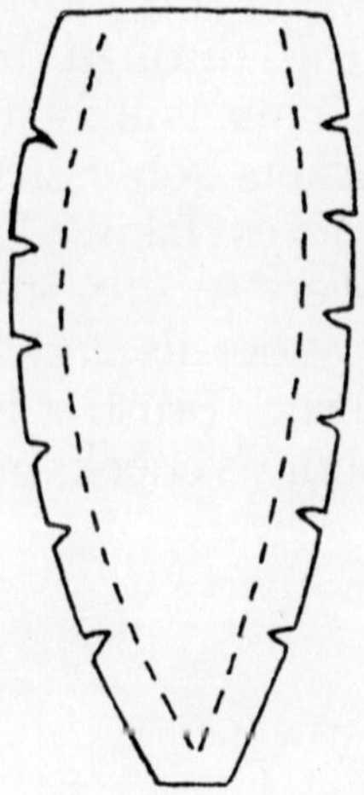

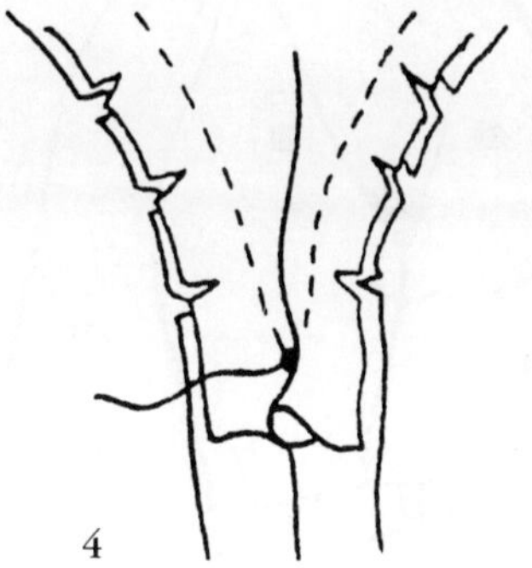

4

Flatten the leg tops to have the seams (which were front and back) aligned. With the heels facing upwards, pit the flattened leg tops side by side in the centre of the lower edge of the front body piece, matching raw edges of the body and legs (6). Place the two body sections together, keeping the legs sandwiched between the two layers. Be sure the arms are aligned. Starting at one neck edge, pin, then stitch, right around the body pieces, taking care with stitching the hands. Leave a 6-7 cm (2½″) gap on one side for the turning and finish stitching at the other neck edge. Do not turn bunny to right side yet.

6

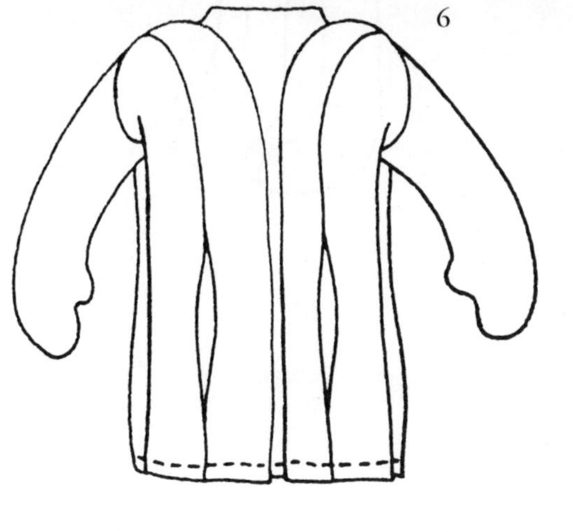

Attach one arm on either side of each body piece, having the top of the arm at the top of the shoulder curve just below the neck seam allowance extension. Be sure the arms are aligned on each body piece, and that you have attached the arms with the thumbs upwards.

Tuck head into neck cavity, having right sides facing and centre front and back matching centre front and back body. Stitch around neck edges, easing the larger neck edge to the smaller one, if this should be necessary. Turn bunny out through turning and stuffing opening.

Stuff arms and pin the front and back together through the arm/body seams. Stitch along this seamline through all thicknesses. This will give movement to the arms. Continue to stuff the body, starting with head. Place stuffing inside bunny in small amounts, distributing it evenly. When body stuffing is complete, close the opening with tiny hand stitches. Stuff legs, then close with opening hand stitches.

Note the illustrations for making grub roses on page 110, and embroider them onto your bunny, wherever you choose. I suggest you place some on the tips of the ears, on the hands and feet and maybe even on the top of the head. Rabbits like wearing lots of roses!

Using pink embroidery floss, embroider the nose with satin stitch and the mouth outline with small chain stitches. Use the 'V' of the centre head piece as a guide for the nose, taking your chain stitches down from the lower point of the nose over the chin seam line for 1.5 cms (⅝″), then stitch the mouth in a line, as illustrated. Using a very strong sewing thread, or dental floss, take your thread through from one eye position to the other. Pull the thread slightly to give the sockets some shape. Stitch on the buttons as eyes, taking lots of stitches to make them very secure. Small hands like to play with toy details and loose buttons are a safety hazard. Brush a little cosmetic blusher onto bunny's cheeks and around her eyes.

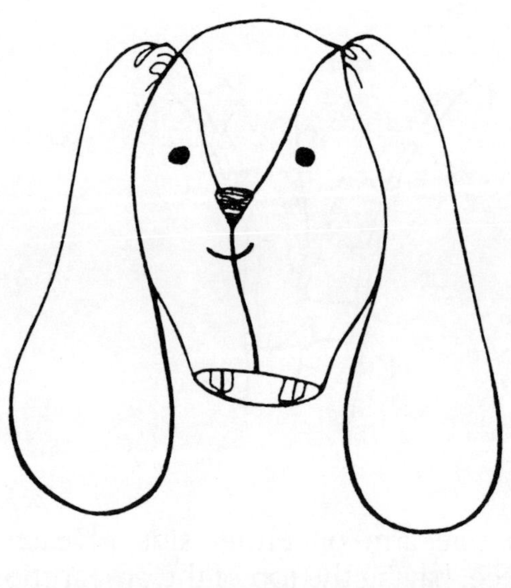

To make the dress and pantaloons

Join each of the two backs to each front at the shoulders, giving two front/back sections. Press open shoulder seams and place the sections together, right sides facing and edges matching. Stitch up centre back openings and around neckline. Turn to right side and press well. Treat these as one layer of fabric from now on.

Tuck the bound edge of the lace underneath the neck edge and stitch in place from the right side, ending lace at edges of back fold-backs (7). Neaten ends of sleeves and the pantaloons and place lace on right sides, edges matching. Stitch just inside the binding, then turn the seam allowance under towards the sleeve, or pantaloons, and stitch from the right side to hold.

7

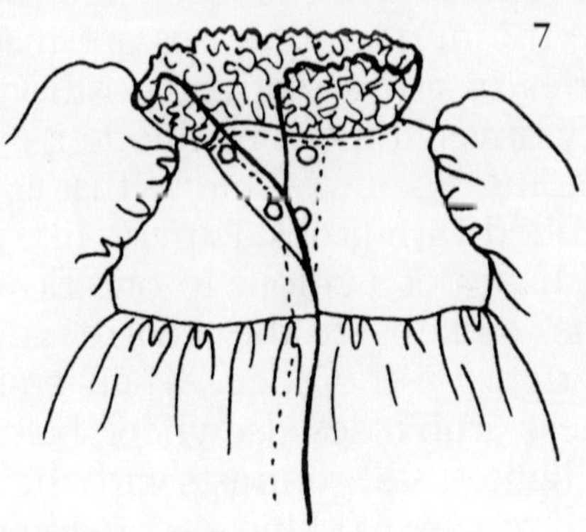

Cut an 8 cm (3¼″) strip from the lower edge of the skirt. Rejoin the pieces enclosing a strip of lace. To do this, place the lace along the edge of the larger fabric piece on the right side, edges matching. Stitch as in the previous step. Place the small strip, right sides facing, over the lace-trimmed edge with edges matching and stitch again, following previous stitching (8).

Finish the lower skirt edge as for the sleeve and pantaloon edges. Gather the sleeve head and stitch the sleeves into the armholes. In continuous seams, stitch from sleeve ends, through underarms and down to waist.

Place (optional) lace along the bodice waist line, on the right side, edges matching. Stitch just inside the binding. Do not turn.

Gather the upper edge of the skirt, pin to waist over previous stitching, adjusting gathers. Stitch, following previous stitching. Turn seam allowance to inside and stitch on right side, as for sleeves, pantaloons and hem. Neaten the back opening edges of the skirt.

Place pantaloon pieces (note there is no side seam) together and stitch down from waist to crotch on both sides. Adjust the pantaloons so that the crotch seams sit directly over one another. Stitch the inside leg seams from one ankle, through crotch and around to the other ankle.

Turn the waist edge over to the wrong side 5 mm (¼″), then again 1.2 cm (⅝″). Stitch along inner fold leaving an opening for elastic insertion. Insert elastic, threading the end onto a safety pin or a bodkin for ease. Try the pantaloons on bunny and adjust the elastic. Hand sew elastic ends together and the opening closed.

8

Try the dress on bunny to adjust the back opening fold-backs. Turn under the back bodice and skirt edges, leaving adequate overlap for press studs (7). Pin, then press when you have decided your fold lines. Stitch down the folded edges. Sew on press studs, having one each at neck and waist, another in-between, and others below the waist on the skirt.

Tie 50 cm (20″) lengths of ribbon in bows around bunny's ears where they meet the head, then hand sew underneath to secure.

Form a large pleat in the ends of the sleeves so that they sit snugly around the wrists. Do not make it so tight that the dress cannot be removed easily. This pleat should be on top for the sleeve, opposite the underarm seam (9). Stitch up about 3-4 cm (1¼″-1½″) from the sleeve edge (not through lace) to secure this pleat. Find the centres of four 50 cm-lengths (20″) of ribbon and stitch these to the wrists at the underarm seam of each sleeve. Fold the pleat around towards the outside and tie the ribbons around the cuff in bows to secure (9).

Tie your wider ribbon around the waist and into a bow at the back as a sash, making thread-carrier loops at the side seams, as required.

Your bunny may like to carry a small cane basket filled with eggs, if desired.

9

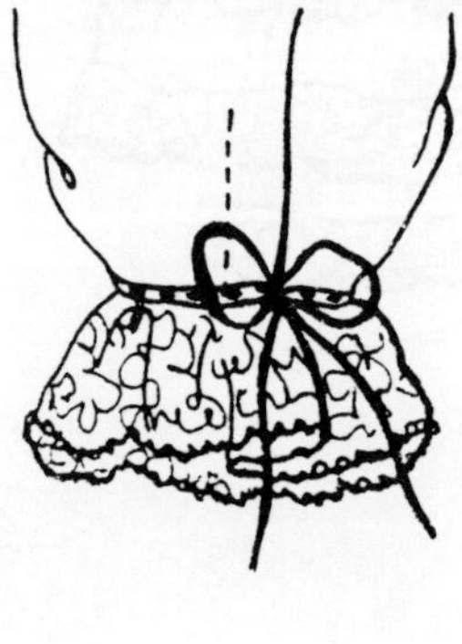

To embroider grub roses

Using two or three strands of embroidery floss, bring thread up through the fabric and make a stitch the length you wish the finished stitch to be, bringing the needle out exactly where the thread initially emerged. Push the needle through almost to the eye. Wind the thread clockwise around the needle six, seven or eight times to make a coil (the theory is that there should be enough thread wound around the needle to make the 'grub' long enough).

Hold the coil down on the fabric with your left thumb, then pull the needle through until the thread is completely through the fabric and the coil, keeping your thumb gently on the coil as you do this. Gently tug the thread back until the coil is laying against the fabric. Re-insert the needle into the right side of the stitch and proceed to make the next grub. Roses are made up of a series of grubs that are positioned so that they dovetail into one another, eventually building up into a circle that is completely filled with grubs. Experts like to use several shades of a colour in one flower — with the darkest in the centre and the lightest right on the edge. When embroidering these grub roses elsewhere, be careful that the lightest still contrasts with the fabric on which you are working — you don't want much of your beautiful work to disappear into the background! Small buds are two parallel grubs emerging from the same hole, with green grubs on either side for leaves.

Make Your Own Bedlinen

Australian-made polyester/cotton sheeting varies in widths, but is usually 250 cm (110″) wide from selvedge to selvedge. Sometimes sheets can be cut with these selvedges at the top and bottom of your sheets. At other times, for different-sized beds, these selvedges are at the sides. Please measure your bed **before** you purchase fabric and be sure that you allow sufficient tuck-in fabric! These instructions will produce linen for any sized bed.

Top flat sheet

Hem the sides and the bottom edge with a 1 cm (½″) double hem. Fold in the top raw edge 1 cm (½″), then again 10 cm (4″). Place fagotting lace — or very wide entre deux lace on the sheet, with its edge against the fold. Zig-zag over the edge of the lace and the fold in the sheet at the same time. Place narrow edging lace against the outer fold so that the edges are butted. Zig-zag over these edges using a narrow stitch. In each case, use thread to either match the lace, or the fabric — do not choose a neutral-coloured thread. You may, of course, plan to make a plain fold back on your sheet, and in this case, simply fold it back 10 cm (4″) and stitch along the inner folded edge.

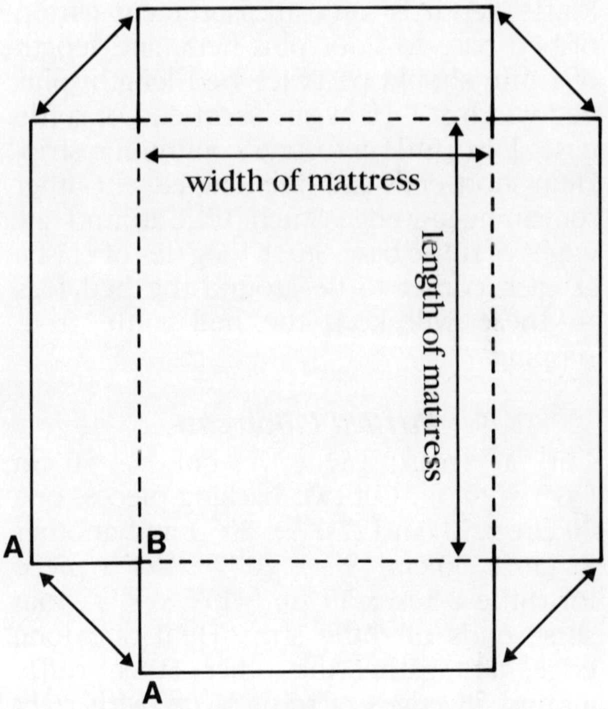

A-B = depth of mattress plus tuck-under allowance

Fitted sheet

See diagram to measure for sheeting. Cut squares from each corner. Join points 'A'. Sew from outside edge to inner corner, forming an angle at each corner of the sheet. Hem around the outside edge, or overlock edges closely. Sew 1 cm (½″) side elastic to seam allowance of each corner seam, using zig-zag stitch and stretching elastic as you stitch. Sew elastic right around sheet edges in the same method.

Quilt cover

If using sheeting, cut one large piece of fabric each for front and back, allowing 12 cm (4¾″) extra on each side of quilt. If using fabric, join pieces, noting pattern matches if necessary, to make up required size front and back. Place front and back together with right sides facing and raw edges matching. Stitch across one short end and both long sides. Press in the open end

1 cm (½″), then 5 cm (2″). Mark and make evenly spaced buttonholes across the opening, and stitch on buttons in corresponding positions, or apply small pieces of Velcro tape across the opening.

Bed ruffle

Quantities for fabrics will depend on how high your bed is off the floor, the size of your bed, etc. The base is the same size as the mattress top, plus seam allowances. Ruffle depth is same measurement as top of bed base to floor plus hem, and length of ruffle should be twice bed length, plus bed width x 2. Hem one short end of ruffle base. Join ruffle into one continuous strip. Hem short ends and one long edge. Gather remaining raw edge. Stitch ruffle around raw edges of ruffle base. Stitch long ties of elastic at each corner to tie around the bed legs — these will keep the bed ruffle from slipping.

Ruffled Pillowcase

Cut a front piece 78 cm x 50 cm (31″ x 20″) . Cut two backing pieces, one 70 cm x 50 cm (27½″ x 20″) and another 22 cm x 50 cm (9″ x 20″) . Cut a piece for ruffle 2.5 m x 10 cm (110″ x 4″) . Join short ends of ruffle strip. Hem one long edge, and gather the other. Stitch ruffle around all edges of front piece, with right sides facing and raw edges matching. Narrow hem one 50 cm (20″) edge of each backing piece. Place the large backing piece over the trimmed front, right sides facing and hemmed edge level with the frill seam stitching. Stitch down long sides and across raw short end. Place the remaining back piece over the large back piece, matching raw edges. Stitch down sides and across top, following stitching line for frill. Turn pillowcase out through open end. The small backing piece becomes the pillow shield.

Plain pillowcase

Cut fabric 50 cm x 1.7 m (20″ x 73″). Turn in raw edges on both short ends. Stitch 1 cm (½″) seam on one end and 5 cm (2″) seam on other. Trim 5 cm (2″) seam end as desired with lace, ribbons etc. Fold fabric as shown in diagram. Stitch down sides, turn pillowcase out and press.

Buttoned pillowcase

Cut one piece of fabric 1 m x 80 cm (45″ x 32″). Fold in a 1 m-long edge (45″) 1 cm (½″), then again 10 cm (4″). Press. On the right side, stitch lace (entredeux or faggotting are suitable) to hold down the hem. One the outer edge stitch lace as for sheet fold-back. Fold pillowcase to have 80 cm (32″) edges even, with right sides facing. Stitch down long edge and across short end. Turn pillowcase to right side. Mark and make 3 buttonholes across the top fold and stitch on corresponding buttons. These pillowcases look good in all sorts of fabric, and are wonderful when made in cotton craft fabrics. Eliminate the lace trim if desired, and simply stitch the hem with straight stitching.

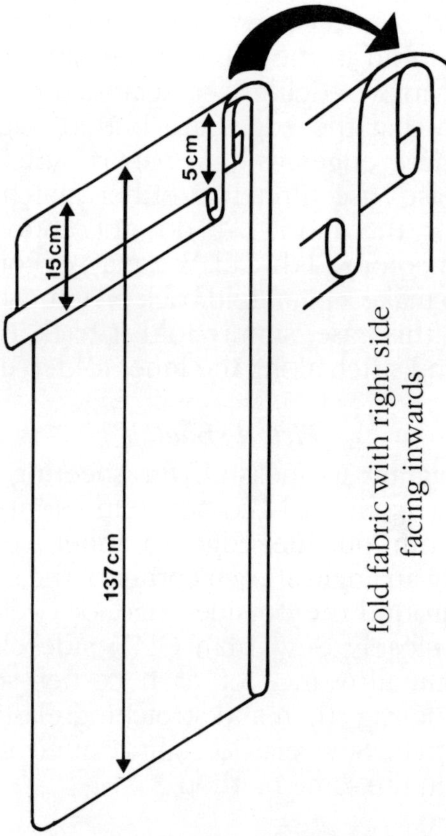

Old-Fashioned Changing Screen

This three-panel screen is easily made by the most amateurish carpenter! It can be any height or width, but you must be sure of stability. I used maple, though pine timber is suitable, but watch for knots in this wood. The screen is identical top and bottom, except that the bottoms of the side supports are not shaped like the tops. Piano hinges hold it together and travel about ⅔ the depth of the screen. I used 5 cm x 2.5 cm (2″ x 1″) side supports and 10 cm x 2.5 cm (4″ x 1″) cross pieces. The wood was sanded well and polished with furniture beeswax, or you could use light tan boot polish, well rubbed in and polished. Use the completed screen to hide an ugly corner in a room — or to create some much-needed privacy.

1. Cut the six side supports to your desired length (1). Cut the six cross supports to the desired length (2).
2. Nail the side supports to the ends of the cross supports (3).
3. Drill holes at the same level in each side support, top and bottom, to take the dowel (4). Make these holes slightly bigger than the dowel's circumference.
4. The dowel pieces slide through the drilled holes. The back and front fabric pieces are joined, top and bottom, with dowel casings (5) formed by two rows of stitching. The area between the seamed edge and the casing forms a ruffle once the dowel is inserted and the fabric pushed into folds.
5. Attach the piano hinges to join the panels, taking care to note which way each panel is to fold. Add fabric bows to tops of fabric panels, if desired.

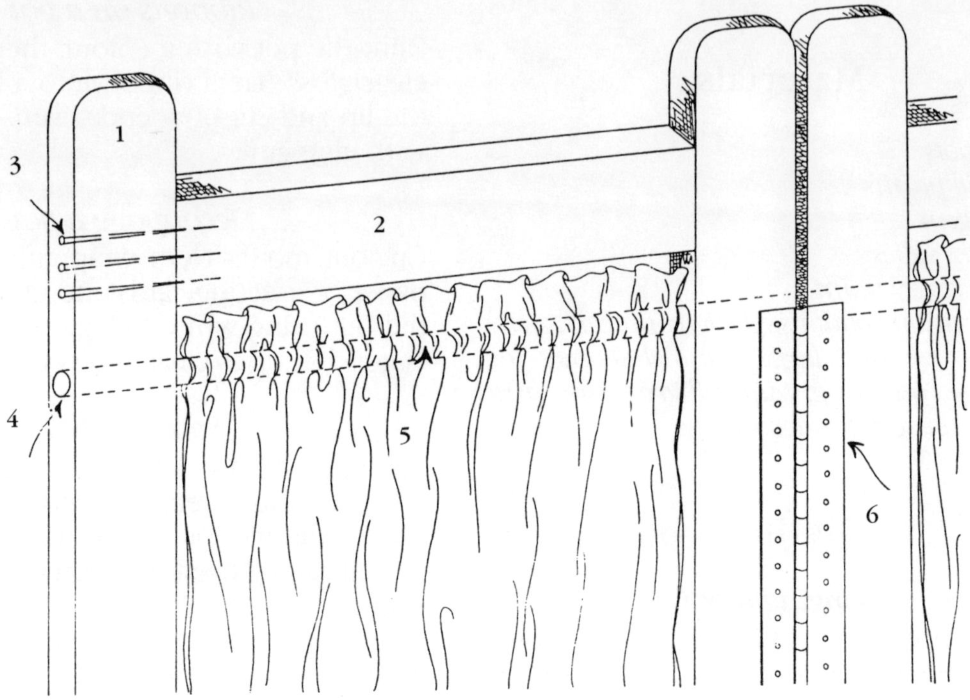

Painted Pots for All Seasons

Basic terracotta pots, or even plastic tubs, can be converted quickly and easily into delightful decorator items. There are dozens of ways you can decorate pots — the following methods can be applied to any pot of any size.

Considerations

Painted pots make good containers or gift baskets. They can serve as desk storage for paper clips or similar items, or you may even wish to fill them with homemade biscuits or chocolates. In this instance, line the inside with cellophane first, tying the ends up over the goodies with a big bow. Given the decorative treatments they will receive, these pots are not suitable for outside use.

Materials

- *Clay pots*
- *Acrylic paints*
- *Glue gun*
- *Paintbrushes*
- *Clear spray paint*
- *Decoration options: Dried flowers, jelly beans, ribbons, large natural sponge for sponge painting, Aquadhere glue and sharp scissors for découpage*

Method

Sponging a pot

Paint the pot with your chosen colour. Pour a small quantity of a slightly lighter colour into a saucer, and dip in the sponge. Have a pad of kitchen towel nearby to blot off excess colour, then proceed to blot the sponge over the pot until the previous colour is covered but still showing through — you're working towards an all-over blotched effect. More than one colour can be layered on, and it's fun to experiment for yourself to achieve interesting colours.

Jelly beans around a pot

Using a glue gun, fasten jelly beans around the outside lip of a pot. Spray several coats of clear paint over the jelly beans to seal them.

Dried flowers on a pot

Sponge the pot in colours to suit the flowers, then glue flowers around the outside lip of the pot using a glue gun.

Ribbons on a pot

Paint the pot with a colour, then paint with clear gloss. Tie a ribbon into a bow around the lip and cut bow ends even. Secure bow with glue gun.

Découpage a pot

Cut out motifs from wrapping paper, wall-paper or greeting cards and glue them onto the pot using white PVA glue — Aquadhere is good. It dries clear and is non-toxic.

Stencil a pot

Acrylic paints are best used with stencils, but you can mix metallic acrylic paints with plain colours for interesting effects. Any stencil can be used, and you may use a small sponge or stencil brush to apply paints. Hold the stencil in place with masking tape while you work. When finished and paint is dry, spray with clear paint to seal.

Painting on Silk

Silk painting has become much easier recently with the advent of new paints and an easy applicator for gutta, the narrow line of paint with which you draw in your design and which also separates the colours while you are painting. There are now endless possibilities for making your own scarves, lengths of fabric, or smaller projects such as cushions.

Materials

- *Lightweight, smoothly woven silk, either 90 cm (1 yd) or 115 cm (45") wide. Wash the silk with Sunlight soap several times to remove natural gum, soak for an hour or two in the soapy water, then rinse well. When dry, it's ready to paint*
- *A frame is necessary to stretch the silk upon. It should be slightly bigger than your finished article. The silk is stretched drum tight across the frame and held with drawing pins*
- *Brushes need only be inexpensive, and in a few sizes*
- *An assortment of silk paints will get you started — say red, blue, yellow and black. From there you can mix colours, purchasing more shades as you need them. Your workplace needs to be flat, and well protected from paint spills*
- *Gutta comes in a variety of colours, including clear, gold and silver*
- *One gutta applicator bottle is essential, but it would be good to have at least two, to keep a bottle for each coloured gutta you use*
- *Gutta solvent is a clear liquid used for thinning gutta*

Method

With your silk in place on the frame, draw in your design. Do this either by tracing off a design held under the silk using either a lead pencil (going over it later with gutta) or your gutta, or draw a design free-hand using gutta. Allow the gutta to dry, but check that there are no gaps in the gutta lines or paint will escape and seep outside your designed areas.

Once your design is finished and the gutta is dry (touch to check) you can start to paint. If the gutta sits on top of the silk and remains sticky, it is too thick, so add some gutta solvent to thin it. It should sink into the silk and form a flat line. You will find through experience how quickly the paint drifts across the silk, and how instantly you seem to have a work of art! The paint will stop right at the gutta, leaving a line between it and the next colour.

Water will help disperse the paint and can thin colours down to be quite light and transparent. When painting is finished, allow to dry on its frame for three to four hours. Place a sheet of white butcher's paper flat, the silk flat on top, and roll the two up and twist the ends around something like a pinwheel. Place this in your vegetable steamer, being sure the water in the steamer does not touch the paper, and that it does not go off the boil or boil dry. Steam for about an hour, then hang to dry. I strongly suggest you make some experimental pieces before embarking on the scarf of your dreams. Whatever you do, you'll have lots of fun!

Paper-covered Pencils and Container

This is a simple project for adults and children alike. The finished tin of pencils would be more than welcomed beside a phone, or on an office desk. As a present for children, you could cover coloured lead pencils and the container with colourful paper.

Materials

- *New pencils*
- *Pretty paper*
- *Empty and cleaned food tin (make sure there are no sharp edges around or inside the rim)*
- *PVA glue*
- *A paintbrush*

Method

Cut 3.5 cm-wide (1½″) strips of paper the length of your pencils. Cut paper to wrap around the tin and overlap at the join. Using the paintbrush, coat the pencils and the tin with glue and wrap the paper around them, adding more glue under the overlap if necessary. Sharpen the pencils when glue is dry. If the noise of pencils clattering into the tin disturbs you, cut a circle of felt and glue it to the inner base of the tin — this will soften the noise!

Plate 13

PLATE 15

PLATE 16

Paper Pricking

There are no expensive tools or materials needed for this craft. The paper can be firm writing paper, and a hand-sewing needle may be all you need to make the pattern.

Considerations

This technique is ideal for personalising writing paper. You may like to monogram the corner, or create borders. Remember to add a touch of pattern to the envelope flap, too. While the usual right side of the decorated paper is smooth, making some perforations from the wrong side — leaving raised edges to the hole on the right side — can be an attractive design feature. Sometimes, old-fashioned punched-paper doilies can be used as a pattern. In this instance, you can follow the intricate patterns to make your own design.

Materials

- *Paper to be decorated*
- *Large embroidery needle with the eye end embedded into a cork; or, a notice-board pin with a firm plastic end for making the holes*
- *Sheet of soft particle board on which to rest paper while decorating*
- *A single hole punch for making larger holes*
- *A pattern from which to copy*

Method

Trace the suggested pattern onto transparent paper, drawing solid lines. Place the paper to be decorated on the particle board, pinning the traced paper over it. Do not push any securing pins through the paper that is to be decorated. Make your pattern by pushing the needle through both layers of paper, following the lines of the pattern and making holes at regular, close intervals. While the holes are sure to become irregular in some places, try to keep them about 2 mm (1/16″) apart.

Decorative Shelf Papers

Materials

- *Firm paper the length of your shelf, and wide enough to rest on the shelf and be folded over to create a decorated front drop*
- *Needle and optional hole punch for making the pattern*
- *Traced pattern of your choice*

Method

Use a glass tumbler, or similar object, to make scallops (or a triangular shape) and design and cut the front drop edge into a pleasing pattern. Make the pattern in the shelf papers as described in the main Method. Fold the shelf papers and put in place. They look terrific in old kitchen dressers.

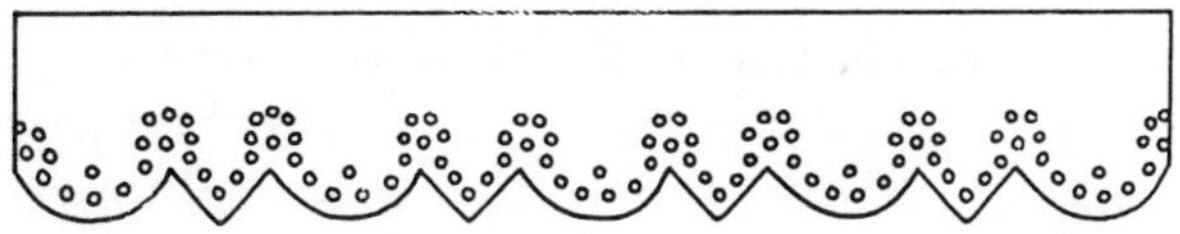

Picture Frames

There are many simple ways of bringing an old frame back to life! There are many sitting waiting to be discovered in junk and opportunity shops right now, or even, perhaps, in your own garage.

Considerations

Don't overlook frames with pictures already in them — it's a simple task to remove all the inside 'bits and pieces'.

Pairs of frames are a good find, and don't hesitate to mix different styles of frames together. Groups of pictures can look very effective and provide an interesting conversation topic. To decide how to group pictures, lay them out on a table, or the floor, and adjust them until the perfect combination is achieved. Measure distances apart and transfer these measurements to the wall. Remember that all frames have different wire, string or chains to hang them by and this will affect just where you have the hook on the wall. White PVA craft glue is used to glue any trimmings to frames, though if covering frames with shells or similar, use a hot-melt glue gun.

Here are some ideas for decorating frames:

Ribbon bands on frames

Glue a band of ribbon around the frame, mitring the corners. Choose a ribbon that fits into a groove of the frame, or use several types of ribbon — the 3 mm (⅛″) wide ribbon would look especially good in small grooves.

Fabric covered wooden frames

Make a paper pattern of the sides and top/bottom of the frame. Allow a tuck-under allowance, but make the mitred corners exact. Cut out the fabric, taking advantage of stripes, borders or motifs you wish to emphasise. Coat the frame with glue, apply the fabric strips and push them into place. Paint fabric with another coat of glue and allow to dry.

Bows at the back of frame

These fabric bows hang behind the picture and can be made from the same fabric as is covering the frame, or from a related fabric. They are simply a long strip that is folded to have right sides inwards and raw edges matching. Angle the ends of the strip, stitch around raw edges leaving an opening for turning. Turn, press very accurately to have seam edge straight and tie into a bow with long tails, or fold strip into a flat bow and add a sewn band to cover the overlaps.

Add a small metal ring at the back of the knot and fix another hook to the wall above the picture hook on which you can hang the bow. Spray starch on the fabric before hanging; this will help the bow to hold its shape. The length of the bow will depend on the size of your frame, but generally the bow is evenly spaced behind the frame. Experiment with scrap fabric before cutting the main fabric. Two small frames hung vertically can look very effective when resting on the same bow.

Other decorative methods

Sponge and/or paint the frame using acrylic paints. Spray paint a frame using glossy pressure-pack paints; glue dried or artificial flowers around the frame, or use wallpaper borders as you would fabric to cover the frame.

Pleated Paper Lampshades

This is a simple solution to covering a circular lampshade quickly. You don't need to fix it in place as the finished shade slips over the top of the existing lampshade and conceals it.

Materials

- *Wallpaper, or wallpaper border, or large sheets of pretty wrapping paper*
- *Optional — ready-pasted lining paper (ie wallpaper lining paper)*
- *Scissors*
- *Bias binding — optional*
- *Paper punch*
- *Braid or ribbon, for holding the top of the shade in place*
- *Ruler*
- *Glue, such as PVA*

Method

Measure the circumference of your shade. You will need a strip of wallpaper that measures 3 times around the circumference of your shade. While the depth of pleats is optional, 2 cm (1″) is about right for most shades. If you're in any doubt about the size of your shade, pleat up a length of lining paper first to see how the pleated shade sits.

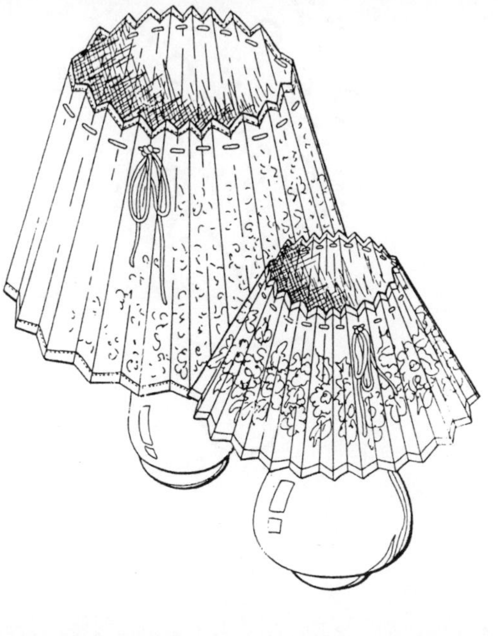

Wallpaper by itself is strong enough to become a lampshade, however, you may wish to line it to make it less transparent and generally stronger. Wrapping papers may need to be lined to make them substantial enough to pleat well. Cut your strip of paper — being sure the sides and short ends are straight. It should be wide enough to cover the existing shade. Moisten the pre-pasted lining paper by running it through a kitchen sink full of lukewarm water, then lay the paper on top and wipe down with a sponge to remove air bubbles and seal the layers together. Trim away excess lining paper and hang to dry. Pleat and/or sew only when completely dry.

If you wish to bind the edges of the shade with bias binding, press the binding in half first and thread your machine with matching thread. I like to bind the edges first, rather than after the paper is pleated. Stitch on the bias, being sure the underneath layer is being caught in the stitching. Some wallpaper borders have 'built-in' borders of colour and do not need bias binding edges.

Start to pleat the paper, like a concertina. Score the edges with your thumbnail, making them sharp and precise. Overlap the ends by tucking/overlapping the edges into the last pleat and glueing — trimming any excess paper away so that the join is concealed and the last pleat appears like the others.

With your paper punch, make holes through the *inner pleats*. Make the holes closer to the inner creases, rather than at the halfway mark or near the outside creases. Thread braid or ribbon through the holes and draw up the pleats so that the lower edge fans out in a circle.

Pomanders

During the Elizabethan era in England things were often, literally, 'on the nose'. Hygiene standards, as we know them, simply did not exist, and the need for scented objects to ward off the offending odours was extremely great! These pomanders are simply citrus fruit studded with whole cloves, which are then allowed to shrink naturally. Only choose perfect fruit — those with broken skin and bad bruises may rot during the drying process, even though cloves are said to be antibiotic. This is truly a portable craft — many a football game has been occupied with studding pomanders — and it's delightful when those sitting near you offer to help. The grandstand smells magnificent!

Materials

- *Citrus fruit, such as lemons, limes and oranges. Grapefruit and cumquats are also suitable, but their sizes may be unsuitable*
- *Whole cloves*
- *Powdered ginger, or ground orris root (both natural preservatives)*
- *Ribbon to trim*
- *A paper bag*
- *A well-hardened thumb!*

Method

Press in the whole cloves into the fruit close to each other until the entire surface has been covered. While the surface is still slightly oily (citrus oil from the fruit's surface seeps out) roll the pomander in either powdered ginger or orris root that has been spread in a saucer. Gently tap off excess powder and place the pomander in a paper bag — not plastic. Allow the fruit to dry naturally over several weeks. It will shrink considerably, drawing the cloves even closer. Tie a bow around the pomander to complete. I keep a bowl of these at the front door all year round — changing the ribbon to tartan for Christmas. You may need to re-roll them in powder from time to time to replenish the perfume.

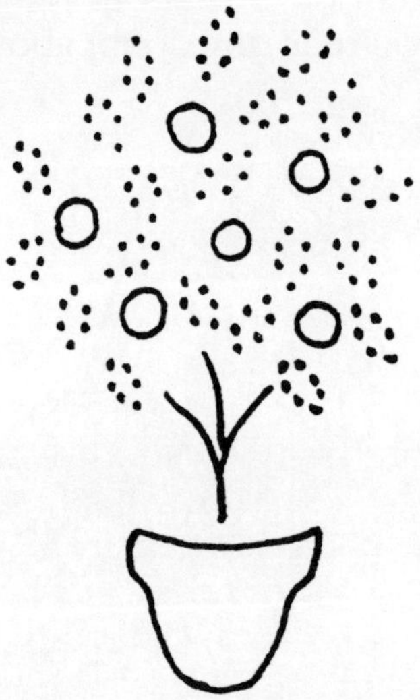

Pot-Pourri-filled Bow

This scented bow can lead many lives. It can be attached to a curtain tie-back, hooked onto a wall, hung inside cupboards to frighten off moths, be tied around the neck of a lamp base or hung behind a picture or a decorative plate. Truly a versatile bow by any standard!

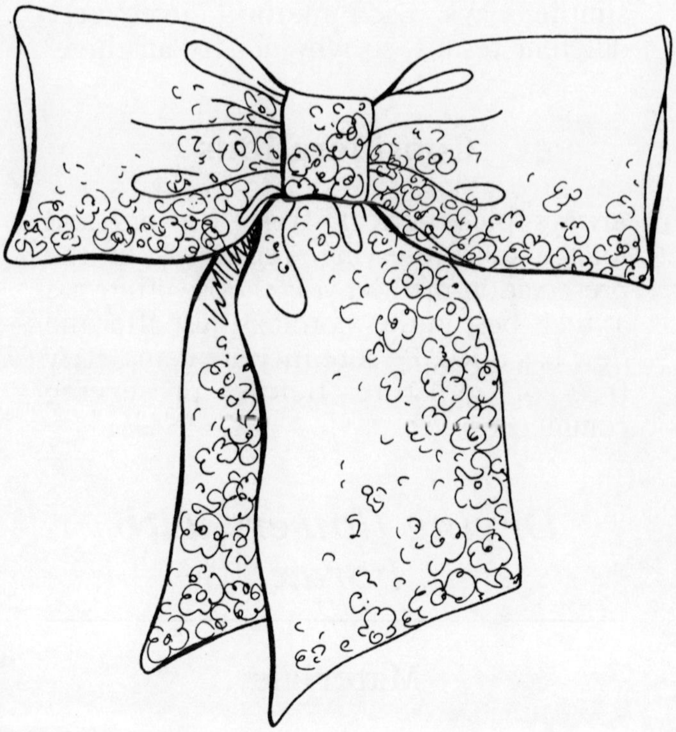

Materials

- *Four x 25 cm (10") fabric squares, cut from your chosen fabrics*
- *Some fine pot-pourri, lavender or rose petal are good as they are not too bulky*
- *A small brass ring for hanging*
- *Sewing thread*

Method

Fold over one square and stitch along the 25 cm (10'') side, leaving a gap opening towards one end. Adjust the seam until it sits in the middle of the piece, press it open with your thumbnail, then stitch across the short ends. Turn the piece through to the right side, but do not press. Fold over two more squares to make tail-pieces. Cut one end of each piece at an angle, then stitch along the long raw edge and angled short end. Leave open the remaining short end. Turn the tail pieces, and press neatly.

Fill the first piece with pot-pourri, closing the opening by hand just before it is completely filled. Fold a fabric scrap into a small band and stitch this around the centre of the pot-pourri-filled piece, crushing it to resemble the centre of a bow. Hand stitch the band at the back to secure. Gather across the top of the two tail pieces and attach these to the back of the filled piece, at the band. Stitch on the small ring at the back if you wish to hang the bow.

Remember that moths hate lavender and that a bow filled with dried lavender will also help chase away mustiness in a cupboard. The warmth from a lamp bulb will help to extract the perfume from a bow hanging from the neck of the lamp base. Perfumed bows hanging on walls will scent the air drifting past, and bows hanging on curtain tie-backs will soon scent the curtains.

Preserved Flowers

Preserved flowers present charming opportunities for decorating. Leaves and flowers take on different appearances as the seasons change, and these changes can be captured easily in three simple ways. Each method gives very different results, so why not try all three?

Considerations

Always pick perfect, fresh flowers and foliage for preserving, regardless of the preservation method you choose. They are at their best in the mornings, just after the dew has dried. Be sure they are completely free of moisture before preserving commences.

Drying flowers with borax

Materials

- *A large, lidded plastic container to hold your selected flowers*
- *Quantity of borax*
- *Small paintbrush*
- *Sticky tape*
- *Clear lacquer (optional)*

Method

Pour a 2 cm (1″) layer of borax across the base of the container, place flowers on layer, keeping them separate from one another. Pour more borax around flowers, brushing borax into crevices and folds until flowers are completely covered but have maintained their shape, and there are no air pockets. Repeat these layers until container is full. Replace lid, seal edges with sticky tape. Leave for one week before checking on the flowers' progress. Use a paintbrush to remove borax remnants from flowers before using. You may choose to spray the dried flowers with clear lacquer to preserve them further.

Using glycerine to preserve firm leaves

Materials

- *Firm leaves on small branches, such as camellias, beech, chestnuts and hawthorns, eucalypts and aspidistras*
- *A cooled mixture of one-third glycerine to two-thirds boiling water*
- *Tall glass containers with narrow necks*

Method

Place about 6 cm (2½″) of glycerine mixture into each jar. Crush the ends of the stems and place stem ends into jars to rest in mixture. Leave in mixture until small droplets of glycerine appear on leaf surfaces. Top up mixture occasionally if needed. Some leaves turn brown, and others take on decorative streaked effects. These leaves are useful for many months and can be used over and over again. Blend them in vases with fresh or dried flowers

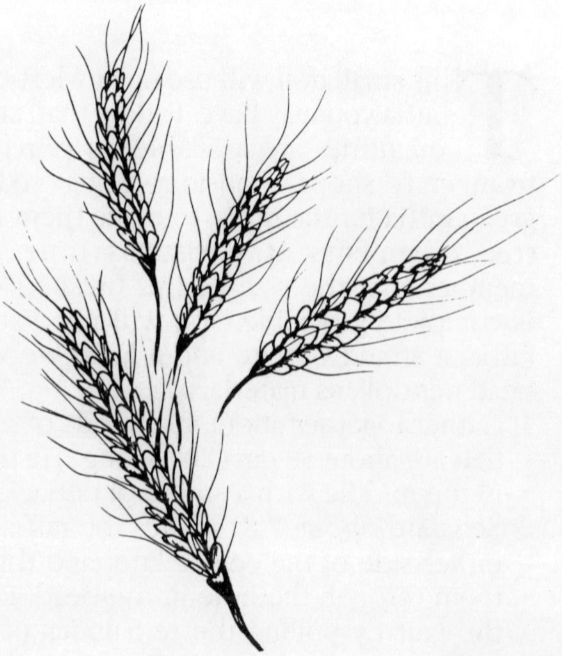

Pressed flowers

Materials

- *Fresh flowers*
- *Blotting paper*
- *Heavy books (disused telephone books are ideal)*
- *Scalpel or sharp craft knife*

Method

If flowers have thick stems, pare some away with a knife or scalpel. Place flowers on two layers of blotting paper, on top or between the pages of a heavy book. Cover with another two layers of blotting paper, close book or place another on top of paper. Weight the flowers even more, perhaps with a brick, and leave for several days before checking. Flowers are dry when they are papery to to touch. Pressed flowers are a lovely addition to personalised writing paper, or arranged into a flat posy to be framed as a picture.

Raffia Doll in Corn Dolly Style

This small doll will use up any left-over raffia you may have. Failing that, small quantities are available for purchase from craft shops. Consider using red or green raffia for the dolls, to make them into tree ornaments at Christmas time. Remember that the size of the finished doll is completely flexible. You will need some raffia, a strand of wire and a large wooden bead per doll, as materials.

1. Gather together about 40 strands of raffia that are about 50 cm (20″) long. Tie them in the middle with a strand of raffia.
2. Separate about 7-8 strands of raffia on either side of the centre knot and thread them through the hole in the bead. Form the hair by pulling the remainder of the raffia strands down around the bead (don't forget the back) to meet the bead raffia, and tie the lot together underneath the bead to create the neck.
3. Plait about 30 strands of raffia to a length of about 20 cm (8″), having the wire inside the plait and not allowing it to protrude beyond the end of the plaiting (if you find that it does, snip it away when the doll is complete). Tie off the ends and unravel the raffia a little, snipping the ends to be level.
4. Halve the main bundle of raffia below the neck, insert the plaited arms, then tie a raffia strand around to create a waist.
5. Divide the remainder of your raffia and bring the strands over each shoulder and tie them criss-crossed at the waist. Trim the end of the skirt to be level. You may like to paint in facial features on the bead. Make a hanging cord if your doll becomes a tree ornament.

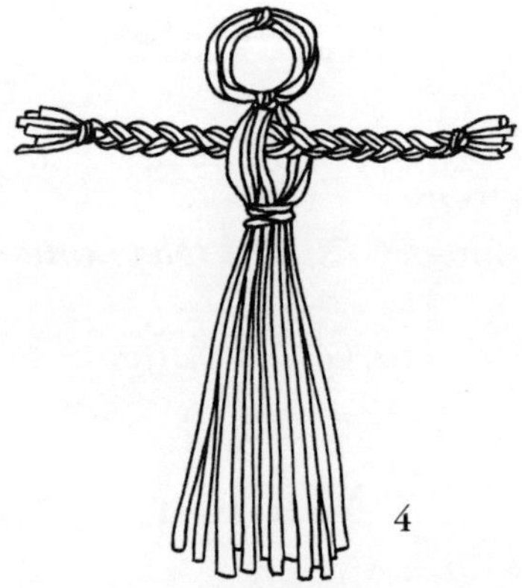

4

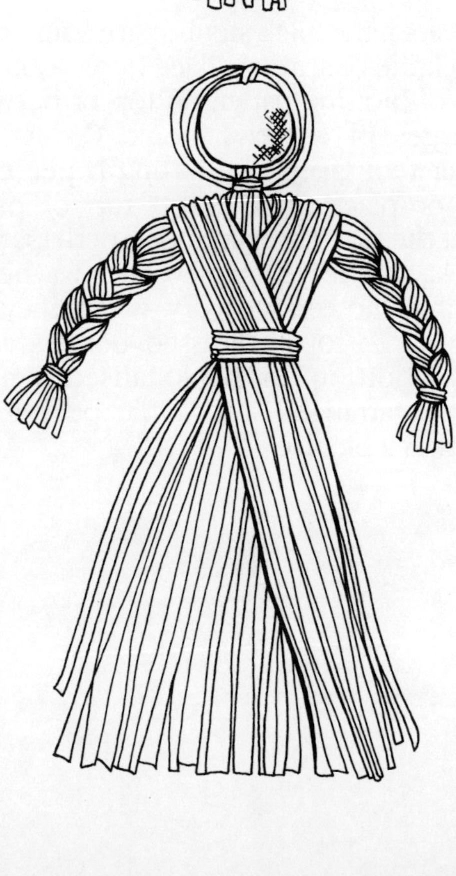

5

1

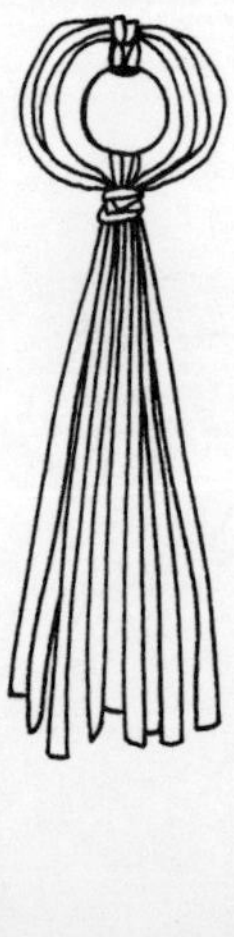

2

3

PLATE 17

PLATE 18

PLATE 19

PLATE 20

PLATE 21

PLATE 22

PLATE 23

Ragging and Sponging Techniques for Walls or Wooden Surfaces

Ragging, like sponging, is a simple painted finish that you can apply to walls and any wooden surface. It is an ideal technique for walls where the surface is imperfect, as the all-over texture tends to disguise any faults. It is a subtle finish, giving warmth and substance to a wall — and it's very inexpensive to achieve.

Considerations

Experiment with colours — the more you discover about colour combinations the more interesting your results will be. I like to use two shades of the same colour, which gives a soft, cloud-like appearance. There is no problem with using colour contrasts, but do practise first to see if you like the boldness of these combinations. There are two methods of Ragging — practice will show you which you prefer to use.

Materials

- *A collection of soft cloths all of the same fabric (for example, use calico, old singlets, sheets or tea-towels). Some people like using scrunched-up plastic bags or plastic food wrap — these too give a pleasing impression, rather like a suede finish. You must use the same fabric throughout the project to create a consistent image because a mix of different weaves and surface textures will look confusing*
- *Two acrylic paint colours of your choice (add white to the main/base colour to create your second colour if working with shades of the same colour)*
- *A wide, shallow container to hold your second colour*
- *A wide paintbrush*
- *Rubber gloves*

Method 1: Ragging on technique

Apply as many coats as necessary of the main/base colour to give a well-covered surface. Allow to dry thoroughly.

Pour the second colour into the shallow container. Immerse the cloth in warm water and wring out. Put on your rubber gloves, open out the cloth and dip it into the paint, making sure it is saturated. Squeeze out any excess and re-shape the cloth into a pleasing bundle that is easy to hold. Start to press the cloth in a slight rolling motion over the base coat, covering it with impressions of the paint-soaked cloth bundle. Rearrange the cloth frequently to avoid a repeated image. Overlap these images slightly to make sure the base coat does not show through too obviously. (If you are using plastic wrap, you will need to dab it onto the base coat, rather than roll it.)

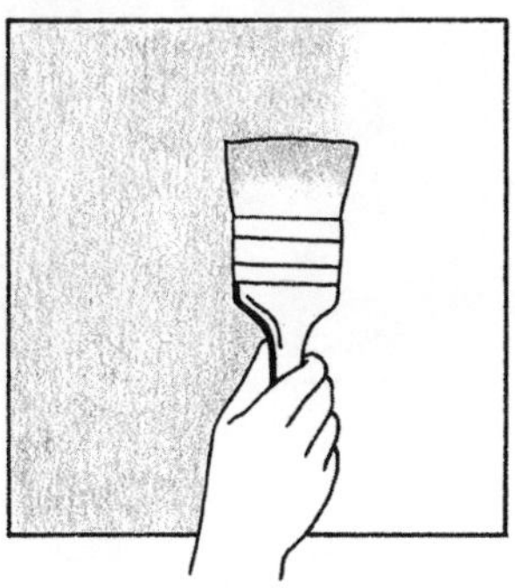

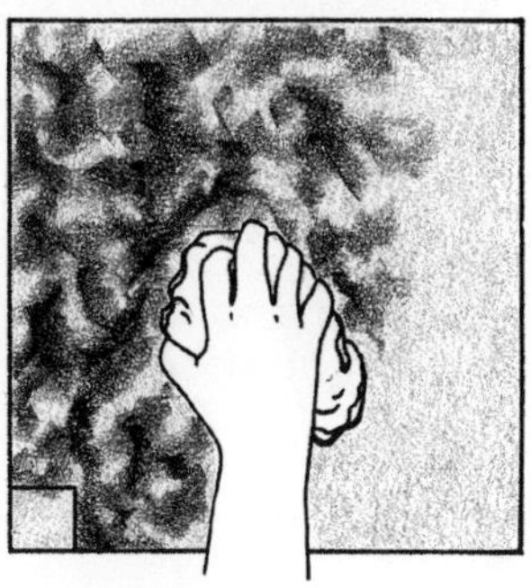

Method 2:
Ragging-off technique

You have to work quickly for this one! If another person works with you, it will save frustration and probably give you a better result. Again, practise this method before using it on your project. Paint the surface with the base coat, as for Method 1. Dilute your second coat with lots of water, and, working in one vertical panel at a time, paint it over the base coat and quickly blot off the paint with dry cloths. You will find that a sufficient amount of the second coat is removed to reveal the base colour underneath. Speed is very important here; if the second coat is allowed to dry (and, therefore, cannot be blotted off) the process is ruined and you will have to start again. Once one panel is complete, continue with the next, trying to avoid overlapping the panels.

If treating a small craft project, such as a tray or a cupboard, with either of these methods, you may wish to seal the finished surface with a gloss paint. These painted techniques provide good backgrounds for folk art or stencilling. They can sometimes be the answer when you need to bring together two colours in a room scheme, using one, or both together in ragging, and later overlaying a stencilled frieze using the two as solid colours.

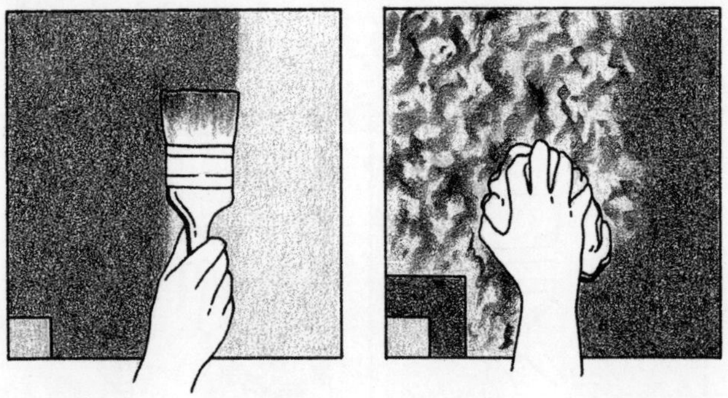

Sponging technique:

1. I suggest you only use a natural sponge — synthetic sponges create rigid lines and are difficult to work with.
2. Paint on two coats of your acrylic paint base coat and allow to dry.
3. Dab your dampened sponge into a shallow tray of colour and wipe away excess paint on kitchen paper. Using even pressure, dab the sponge over the painted surface, creating an even and subtle effect.
4. If you want to add another colour, repeat the process using a cleaned sponge. Remember to experiment first with two-colour sponging, as the results may surprise you!

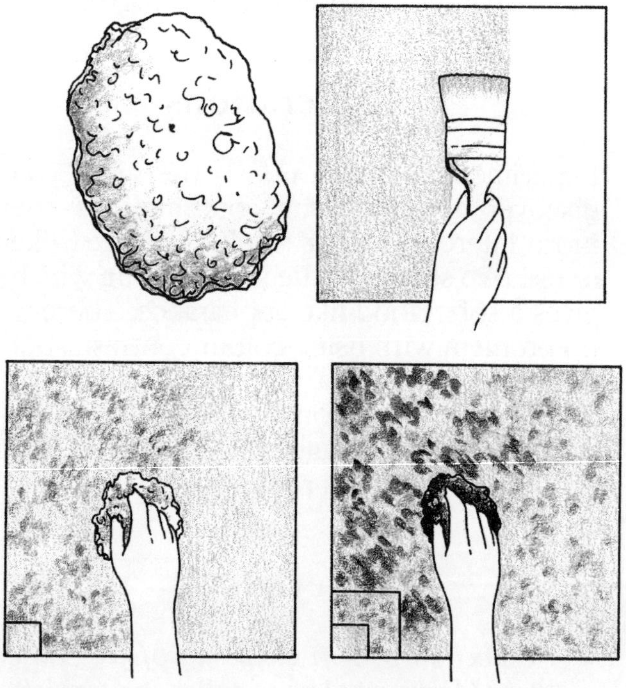

Scrunchies

These simple-to-make hair trims cost very little. They are good for hair because they hold it gently in place. They can become an accessory which matches your clothing. Anyone with long hair will bless you when they find these in their Christmas stocking!

Material

- *Size is flexible, but a piece of fabric 15 x 40 cm (6″ x 16″) is adequate*
- *Elastic — a long piece to start with. Do not cut into lengths*
- *Sewing thread*

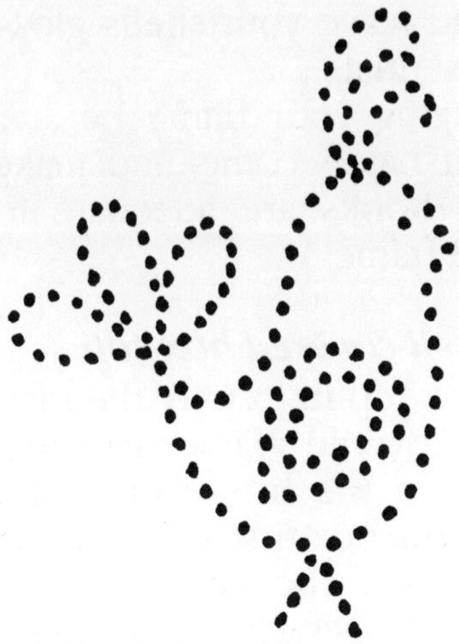

Method

Fold in one 15 cm (6″) end to wrong side and press. Fold over the fabric lengthways with right sides facing and edges matching. Pin one end of the elastic to the centre of the unfolded end. Stitch across the short end, securing the elastic end as you stitch. Pivoting at the corner, stitch down the long side. Do not stitch across the folded end.

Using a blunt knife, a chopstick or similar, turn the fabric tube inside out by inserting the knife at the stitched end and pushing this end through to the other end. With the scrunchie now turned, neaten the long stitched edge by 'thumb pressing' the edge to be even; do not make a crease on the opposite long edge.

Pull up the elastic so that the fabric puckers up to about 22 cm (9″) and tuck the stitched end inside the open folded end, allowing the elastic to protrude. Stitch twice across through all thicknesses to secure and then trim off the elastic close to the stitching.

Shell-covered Picture Frame and Box Top

If you collect shells, as I do, these projects may provide some very special decorative items for your home. They'll be covered in pretty shells that are sure to remind you of the holidays when you found them!

Materials

- *Shells of varying sizes and colours*
- *Hot-melt glue gun*
- *Bare frame of any size and shape (though it is possible to decorate an already existing mirror or framed picture)*
- *Bucket of warm soapy water to wash the shells*

Method

Wash, rinse then dry your shells. Sort them into sizes — small, medium and large. Obviously, the very largest may not be suitable for your frame as it may be too heavy or awkward to secure — you should judge this proportion for yourself. I have found it's best to keep the largest shells at the corners, or have them evenly spaced in the middle of the sides, or have one large focal point at the lower centre edge. Examine your shells and be aware of any damaged areas. Aim to have these concealed when the shells are in place.

Glue guns operate by electricity and when in use push out thick liquid glue that is extremely hot. The glue dries very quickly and is capable of holding quite heavy objects in place very efficiently. Please take care not to get the glue on your hands while it's hot — it may burn. The glue dries clear and you will soon judge how much to use on each shell.

Heat your glue gun and start to plan where you will glue your shells. Glue on the largest shells first then, by overlapping or butting them together, continue glueing shells into place until the frame is covered. The more irregular they appear, the better the frame will appear. Tiny shells can be glued on top of larger shells and tucked into empty crevices. You may wish to give your finished frame a spray with clear gloss paint to seal it, and leave your shells glossy, but this is not essential.

When hanging your frame be aware of how heavy it has become, and make sure the hanging hooks are adequate for the weight of the frame.

Shell-covered box top

Treat your box top in exactly the same way as the shell-covered frame, keeping your largest shells in the lid's centre. You may wish to paint the box first and, if so, perhaps you could finish the surface by lightly pressing on paint using a natural sea-sponge. You may wish to seal the box and shells with a lightly sprayed-on coat of clear gloss paint.

Silk Pearl Bag

When it comes to storing your precious pearls, nothing does it better than pure silk fabric. Pearls and silk are very compatible, and the soft fabric certainly protects the pearls from any abrasive surfaces. I have used pieces of thick silk brocade to make this drawstring bag but, if this is not available to you, consider quilting some thinner silk before making it into your bag. Always use a fine silk as lining — not a synthetic fabric.

Materials

- *2 pieces 30 cm x 22 cm (12" x 8½") from main silk fabric and two identical pieces from silk lining*
- *3 m (3¾ yd) of silk or acetate cord for drawstring and bag edging*
- *Sewing thread*

Method

Round off two corners of each lining and each main fabric piece on a 22 cm (8½″) edge, using the rim of a glass as a guide, so that each piece is identical. Place the lining pieces together in pairs, with right sides facing and stitch around the edges, leaving the top open. Repeat this step with the main fabric pieces. Turn the main fabric bags to the right side.

Mark in and work two horizontal buttonholes on each main fabric piece, 8 cm (3¼″) down from the top and 3 cm (1¼″) in from each side.

With right sides facing, pin together the top raw edges of the lining bag to the main bag, aligning the seams and the raw edges. Stitch around 1 cm (½″) from the raw

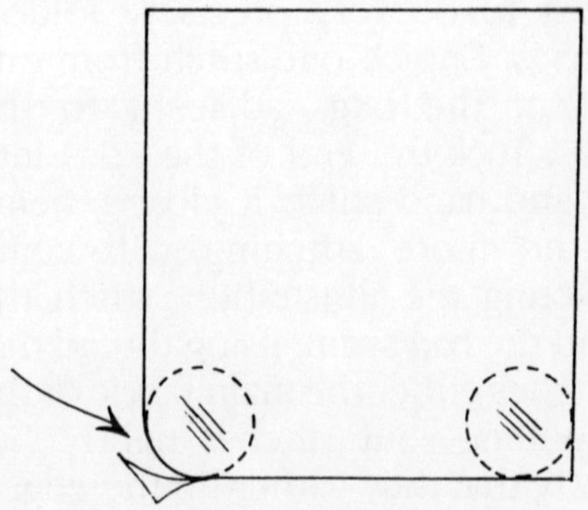

1. Cut away the corners using a kitchen tumbler as a guide

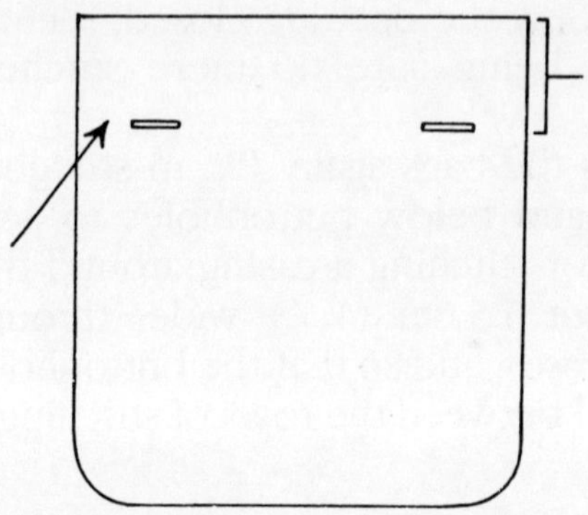

2. Make the horizontal buttonholes in from the edges and top

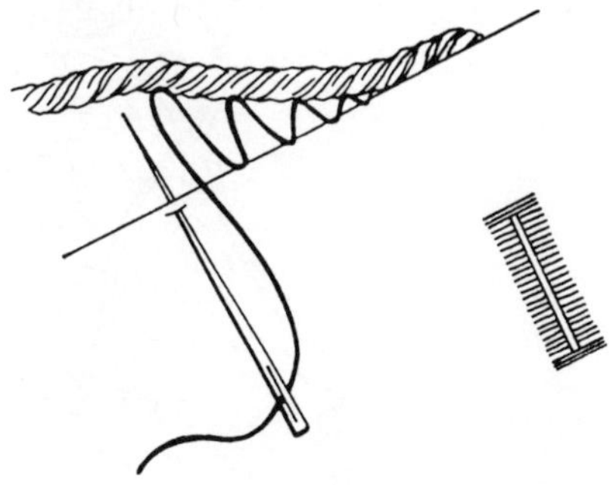

3. Tuck the cord into the side seam level with the buttonhole and stitch on the bag's edge as shown

edges, leaving a gap of approximately 6 cm (2½″) for turning. Turn the bags to their right sides through the opening and then push the lining down into the main fabric bag.

Hand sew the turning opening closed and 'thumb crease' the seam line where both fabrics meet to be very precisely folded. Press the bags. Unpick one stitch from one side seam of the bags adjacent to the buttonholes. Tuck the end of the cord into this cavity and hand stitch it closed, being sure that no more stitching will come undone. Noting the illustration, stitch the cord around the bag seam, using thread that closely matches either the main fabric or the cord and pulling your stitches tightly, but not so tightly that they gather up the edges. When the cord reaches around to be adjacent to the other buttonhole, unpick one more stitch from the seam and cut the cord, allowing 1 cm (½″) to tuck into the cavity. Sew the opening closed, securely as before, being sure no more stitches will undo.

Press the bags again. Pin in straight lines above and below buttonholes to act as a guide for stitching a casing around the bag of about 1.5 cm (½″) wide, through all thicknesses, and so that the buttonholes are centred between the rows of stitching.

Cut the remaining cord into four equal pieces. Using a bodkin or a safety pin through the cord end, take one piece through one buttonhole, along the casing, out and then back through the buttonholes on the opposite side, then through the remaining casing section and out the last buttonhole. Repeat this process with the remaining piece of cord for each bag, starting at the opposite side to the first cord. This gives you two cord ends on either side. Even up the ends, knot them together about 3 cm (1¼″) from the ends, and then unravel the cord to form a tassel-like trim. Cut the unravelled ends to be even. Pull on both knotted ends to close the bag.

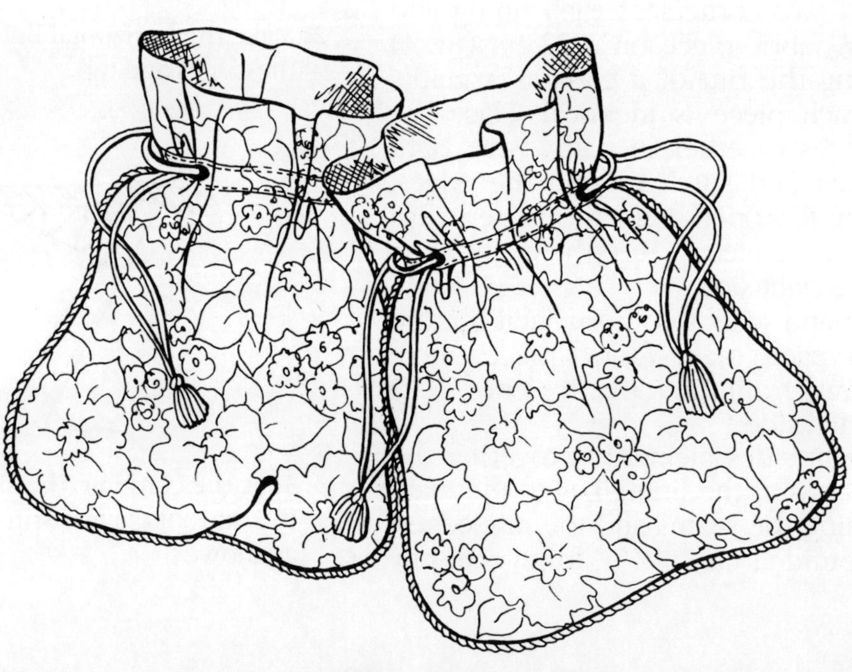

4. Finished bags

Small Bear in a Bag

This is a very easy bear to make and has the potential to become a lifelong companion. His 'Very Useful Bag' is one of his favourite possessions, and he loves to be carried around in it as bears generally like to sleep a lot.

Materials

- *50 cm (2') of plain cotton, quilter's muslin or home spun for bear and bag*
- *60 cm (2") of patterned fabric for ears, paws, soles, hearts and side bag pieces*
- *2 m (2½ yds) of cord for bag drawstrings*
- *Four large (about 2 cm (1") across) buttons for joints*
- *Two safety eyes*
- *Scraps of iron-on interfacing for heart appliqué*
- *Sewing thread, and suitably coloured thread for appliqué*
- *Linen thread, or similar strong thread for the joints*
- *Embroidery thread for the facial features and hearts*
- *Long doll-making needle*
- *300 gms (10 oz) of polyester fibre for stuffing*

Method

Sewing suggestions: All seam allowances are 6–8 mm (¼") (or the width from your needle to the edge of your machine presser foot is ideal — line up the foot edge with the fabric edge and this width will occur). Stitch curves and pressure points twice for strength. Clip seam allowances through to just short of the stitching to allow for ease when turning and stuffing. For added strength, turn your machine to a slightly shorter stitch length than you usually use — say 1¾–2.

Cut out the pattern pieces as shown on the pattern sheet at the back of the book.

Cut out the pattern pieces as shown on the pattern sheet at the back of the book. For Bear: Cut two front bodies, two back bodies, four arms, four legs and two ears from plain fabric. Cut two ears, two soles, two paws and a 60 cm x 10 cm (2' x 4") strip for neck bow.

For Bag: Cut a 12 cm x 65 cm (5" x 2½") strip from plain fabric, and two strips 10 cm x 65 cm (4" x 2'2") from patterned fabric for side strips. Instructions for cutting out hearts from pattern fabric follow in appliqué section.

1. Mark in the darts on the wrong side of the head, and the facial features on the front pieces — see illustrated pattern pieces. Mark in the darts on the lower back body. Mark where ears are to be stitched. Place plain ears together with patterned ears, and legs together in pairs. Note illustration, then pin and stitch patterned paws onto arms. It does not matter onto which end of the arm you pin — they are identical.

2. Sew the darts at the top of the body fronts, and press the darts downwards. Sew the body front sections together at the centre front. Stitch around the curved edge the ears. Clip seams and turn to right side. Stuff ears with a very small amount of fibre. Baste ears into position on fronts at markings, matching raw edges.

3. Stitch darts in the lower body backs, pressing open the dart seam allowances. Stitch body back sections together leaving an opening for stuffing in centre back, as illustrated. Ease stitch around the back lower body with a gathering stitch. With

right sides facing and edges matching, pin body back and front together, pulling up ease-stitching to fit front to back. Stitch around edges, then turn out to right side through stuffing opening. Fold neck tie over double lengthways, raw edges matching. Cut each end at an angle and stitch around the raw edges, leaving an opening in the centre for turning. Turn, press edge seam neatly.

4. Press patterned paws down onto arms. Place arms together in pairs and stitch around edges, leaving opening at upper arm back for turning and stuffing. Clip seams and turn to right side. On leg pairs, stitch from toes around to heels, leaving an opening at upper back for turning and stuffing — do not stitch across straight lower edge. Tie off stitching at toes and heels securely. Clip around straight lower foot edges at 1-cm (½″) intervals to a depth just short of your seam allowance. Pin the soles to these clipped edges, fanning out the leg seam allowance to fit. When satisfied with fit, stitch and turn legs out to right side.

5. Push domed button part of safety eyes through front at markings — you may have to snip through the fabric very slightly to do this. Connect the safety ring to each eye by pushing the ring over the shaft of each eye. The points at the centre of the safety ring face away from the dome. Stuff legs, arms and body with fibre. Take your time doing this, making sure bear is firmly stuffed and not lumpy or uneven. When complete, close stuffing openings by hand with small stitches — see page 8 for ladder stitch — using double thread in your needle.

6. Thread linen thread onto your doll needle and knot ends together. Take a small stitch to secure ends at one arm or leg 'X' on the body. Take the thread through and back through the button, then take the needle and thread through the body at the 'X' and out at the opposite 'X'. Stitch through and back through the opposite button, then take the needle back through the body and complete the first button, pulling the thread very firmly. Take the needle back through the body again and complete the second button, securing the thread under the second button. Repeat this process with the remaining two limbs and buttons. Be sure to stitch these limbs on securely as your bear will come in for a lot of love and attention!

7. Using three strands of brown embroidery thread, use satin stitch to make the nose and small chain stitches to make the mouth smile. Trace off the small heart motif and cut out the shape to use as a pattern. Transfer the shape to the bear's left front, and using small chain stitches and three strands of red embroidery floss, embroider the heart. Fill in the heart with a continuous row of stitches. Tie the neck tie around your bear's neck and into a bow.

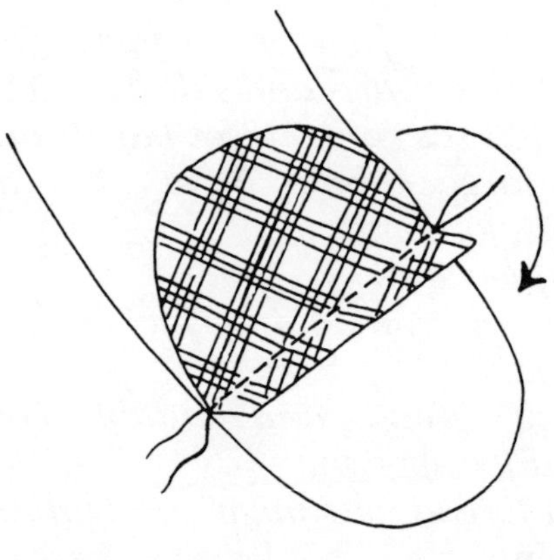

CALICO AND SMALL BEAR'S ARMS AND PAWS

8. **Machine appliqué**:

Step A. Iron interfacing onto the patterned fabric for the appliqué hearts, using a medium-heat iron and having the fabric closest to the iron. The grainy side is the interfacing's glue side. Trace off and cut out the large heart motif to use as a pattern and draw two heart shapes onto the interfaced surface of the patterned fabric, so that the patterned fabric is on the bias. Cut these heart shapes out very neatly. Trace off and cut out the large heart motif to use as a pattern and draw two heart shapes on the interfacing side of the patterned fabric, so that the patterned fabric is on the bias. Cut these heart shapes out very neatly. Centre, pin and baste them so that the top dip in the upper heart sits 9.5 cm (4″) from the upper raw edge of the centre muslin piece of the bag. The top dip in the lower heart sits 10.5 cm (4¼″) from the same point in the upper heart.

Step B. Using toning sewing thread, turn your machine to a narrow zig-zag stitch and stitch around over the heart edges very neatly, starting at the upper dip. Trim away any stray threads, then turn your machine to a slightly wider stitch, and close up the stitches so that they form a satin stitch. Stitch around the hearts again so that the original zig-zag stitching is completely covered.

Hand Appliqué: Follow *Step A* instructions for machine appliqué. Thread an embroidery needle with three strands of red embroidery floss. Using blanket or buttonhole stitch, embroider around the heart's edges. Your stitches should be reasonably close together, and evenly spaced.

9. Stitch the two patterned fabric strips down either side of the appliquéd centre piece, taking the same seam allowances as you did for the bear. Overcast the outer and upper edges of the bag. Fold the bag across in the middle at what will be its base, right sides facing and raw edges matching. Stitch down the sides, starting your stitching 3 cm (1¼″) below the top raw edge. Turn in the unstitched portion's edges (on both sides of the bag) the same width as the seam allowance, and stitch each one back to secure. Fold the upper edges over and inwards 1.5 cm (¾″) and press, then stitch across at the overcast edge to create the cord casing.

10. Cut your cord into two equal pieces and, using a bodkin or something similar (a safety pin or a bobby pin are good substitutes), thread one cord through one side and right around and out the other casing hole on the side you started. Thread the remaining cord through in the same way, starting at the opposite side — see illustration. Even up the ends of the two pieces of cord and knot them together, unravelling the ends, then trimming the frayed threads to be even like a tassel. Place the bear into the bag and pull on the two knotted ends. The neck of the bag will close around the bear's neck.

Safety note: If you do allow a small child to play with this bear, please be sure to stitch on limbs, and any other trimming, strongly and with extreme care, to avoid accidents.

Small Christmas Puddings

These small puddings require no cooking, and make good presents when boxed imaginatively. They keep for weeks in the 'fridge and are a terrific replacement for chocolates at the end of a meal. Given that the consistency of tinned Christmas puddings varies from one brand to another, there are some ingredient options with this recipe.

Ingredients

For puddings

- *One 500-gram (1 lb) tin of Christmas pudding*
- *125 grams (4 oz) of Copha (half a usual block)*
- *Spirits, such as Whiskey, Brandy or Rum (Optional)*
- *Cocoa (optional)*
- *Small paper cup-cake or chocolate containers*

For icing and trimming

- *1½ cups icing sugar*
- *One egg white*
- *Lemon juice*
- *Plastic or freezer bag*
- *Fake stemmed cherries, or segments of glacé fruit*
- *3 mm-wide (⅛") ribbon*

Method

Crumble the pudding into a basin until it is well broken up. Melt the copha over a low heat and cool slightly. Pour into the pudding and mix well. Add a generous tablespoon of spirits and mix again. Take out about a tablespoon of the mixture and roll into a ball, adjusting so that it will end up big enough to fill your containers, and so that the consistency is not too moist. Bear in mind that the copha will set firmly once cool. If too moist, add a little cocoa. Continue to roll into smooth balls and place each into a paper or chocolate container. Set aside to firm.

Meanwhile, separate the yolk from the egg white, and beat the white into a frothy consistency. Add the sifted icing sugar and a few drops of lemon juice and beat until mixed. You should have icing that is glossy and which is similar to very thick, runny cream. Spoon the icing into the plastic or freezer bag and snip off a small amount of one lower corner of the bag. Squeeze icing through this corner, forming mounds that sit on the top and sides of each pudding. Take care with decorating your puddings, as the icing does not set quickly. Practise first if you wish!

Add a cherry, or piece of fruit to the top of each pudding, or tie a small bow around each pudding, just above the top of the paper or chocolate container. Keep refrigerated until used. Will keep well (while refrigerated) over the festive season.

Smocked Baby's Gown

Smocking has come a long way from being the first 'elastic' in the simple gowns worn centuries ago by men and women, to being the beautiful embroidery craft it is today. It is most effective when stitched on babies' clothes, and it seems smocked baby dresses inevitably become family heirlooms, so choose a quality fabric with this in mind.

Materials

- *2 m (2½ yd) of 115 cm-wide (45") wool/cotton blend fabric, or cotton voile*
- *Embroidery threads as desired, for smocking and embroidered flowers*
- *Smocking dot transfer, or a fabric marker and ruler to make smocking dots*
- *Three small press studs for back closure (or substitute buttons and buttonholes)*
- *2.3 m (90") fine cotton lace to match fabric*
- *Strong sewing thread to pull up smocking gathers*

Method

Trace off the pattern pieces from the pattern sheet at the back of the book. Lay out your fabric and cut out one front skirt, two back skirts, two sleeves, one front yoke and two back yokes. Cut a 30 cm (12") length of 5 cm-wide (2") bias to finish the neckline. Overcast the edges of all pieces. Apply lace to the lower edges of the sleeves, noting the illustration, or turn up and hand sew a narrow hem. If applying lace, lay it down on the right side of the fabric, about 3 mm (⅛") in from the raw edge, then zig-zag to secure. The machine's action rolls the raw fabric edges over onto the lace and encloses the edges. Press the small roll away from the lace and on the right side, stitch a holding stitch through the fabric and lace right at the edge of the fabric.

If using a smocking dot transfer, iron it into place where required on the wrong side of the fabric. If using a marking pen, use a ruler to mark evenly spaced dots in rows. Stitch your dots, then gather up smocking rows on the upper edge of the skirt front and the lower edge of the sleeves, leaving room at the wrist for a frill to form below the smocking.

Unpull the gathering from each end of the skirt's gathered panel until about 5 cm (2") of flat fabric shows either side. Cut the armholes from the front piece, using the back dress piece armhole as a pattern. Readjust your gathers so that the front skirt is about 2–3 cms (1"-1¼") wider than the front yoke. This extra length allows for 'shrinkage' during the embroidery stage. Tie the thread ends together securely in pairs or threes close to the start of the gathers. These gathering threads are snipped and removed when all smocking and embroidery is finished. Unpull the gathering threads from either end of the sleeve's gathered panels until about 4–5 cm (1¾"-2") of flat fabric shows on either side. Draw up the threads evenly until they sit together firmly, then tie them off, as for the dress front. Proceed to smock the sleeves and the upper front skirt as desired following directions in 'Smocking' and noting stitch illustrations.

Seam allowances are 1 cm (½") for the dress, and 8 mm (¼") around the neckline. Seams for shoulders, underarms and side seams should be French seams (see illustration). Pin your smocked panels onto your ironing board, embroidery side down, being sure that the stitching and pleats are sitting 'straight'. Hold a steam iron just above them and allow the steam to penetrate the fabric. Allow the smocked panel to cool while it is still pinned, then remove the panel and check it against the width of the front yoke. It is possible to stretch the panel slightly to fit by re-steaming it in a stretched position and allowing it to cool. If your panel is slightly too long, ease it into place as you stitch. Some fullness will not hurt.

Stitch the front yoke to the smocked skirt, having your stitch line directly above the top rows of smocked cable stitch. Gather across the upper back yokes slightly and attach to the basic yokes. Attach front and back at shoulders. Gather around sleeve caps and insert sleeves into armholes, right sides facing and raw edges matching.

Stitch the skirt backs together from hem, stopping 10 cm (4″) from skirt/yoke seamline. Press seam allowance and yoke facings to one side, forming a fold line in the left back yoke for the facing/turnback. Neaten the edges of the facing and the underlay.

Fold the binding strip in half lengthways, matching raw edges. Press, as shown, into a gentle curve. Pin, then baste this around the neckline and over facing/turnback upper edges with right sides facing and raw edges matching, allowing it to extend 6 mm (¼″) beyond the neckline at each end. Stitch around near basting. Trim seam allowance to 3 mm (⅛″) and clip into allowance to create ease. Fold in the narrow ends of the binding, then turn folded edge of binding over to wrong side and hand sew the fold to the row of machine stitches. Stitch the underarm and side bodice and skirt seams in continuous French seams. Stitch lace around the hem of the dress, following the same process as for the sleeves, overlapping lace ends and neatening edges by hand. Attach your machine's twin needle, and make five, or more, evenly spaced rows of twin needle tucks around the hem. Use your machine's presser foot for your guide for evenly spaced rows, butting the edge of the foot against the previously stitched row, then stitching.

Make bullion stitch roses across the yoke and above the tucks, if desired, using darker pink in the centre with the lighter shade at the edges. Work leaves either side of roses, using lazy daisy stitch. Or, make small French knots around in the sleeve's narrow hems, placing knots about 6 mm (¼″) apart, if desired. You may like to make similar knots around the neckline, close to the seamline on the right side. Hand sew the press studs to the back opening, or sew on buttons and make corresponding buttonholes.

Smocking

All embroidery is worked with two strands from the thread and, for your ease of work, try to embroider using thread lengths of around 50 cm (20″). The top row of gathering on the dress front, and the row closest to the wrist on the sleeves, are meant only to hold the gathers securely while stitching. Commence cable stitch above the next row down.

RED AND NAVY EMBROIDERY VERSION

This design uses only cable stitch in the smocking, which is worked into straight rows of cable stitch and stacked triangles. Small pairs of bullion stitches are worked at the base of the design, each pair surrounding a small French knot. Each triangle takes up ten pleats across, with one pleat between each triangle. There are nine triangles across the front of the dress. Each border of cable stitch is two rows of stitching deep, and each triangle is four rows of stitching deep.

Start by finding the centre pleat of your gathered skirt panel, and allocate the centre ten pleats for your centre triangle. Stitch this centre triangle in red then, missing one pleat, stitch blue triangles either side. Continue to miss one pleat between each triangle and stitch alternate red and blue triangles across the dress front. Stitch another panel of triangles below the first row, alternating the colours. Any pleats not embroidered at the sides can be eased out when the gathering threads are snipped and removed.

Stitch a panel of cable stitch, two rows deep, across the gathers below the top two rows of triangles. Repeat another two rows of triangles, then stitch the **bullion stitch** pairs between the lower triangles, taking them across three pleats (with the one pleat left between each triangle becoming the centre pleat in each bullion stitch). Stitch a **French knot** in the centre of each pair of bullion stitches.

The sleeves have a cable band nearest the hemmed edge. There are three triangles across each sleeve and the sleeve embroidery is one triangle less deep than it is on the dress front. There are two pairs of bullion stitches with a French knot centred in each at the base of the sleeve smocking.

PINK EMBROIDERY VERSION

This is stitched with a band of four rows of cable closest to the top of the skirt panel, and the remainder of the embroidery is rows of diamond stitch (sometimes called chevron stitch) that form a trellis pattern. A diamond stitch is worked between two rows of gathering, from one row down to the next. The sleeve smocking is not as deep, being only five rows of diamond stitch, but otherwise identical to the dress front.

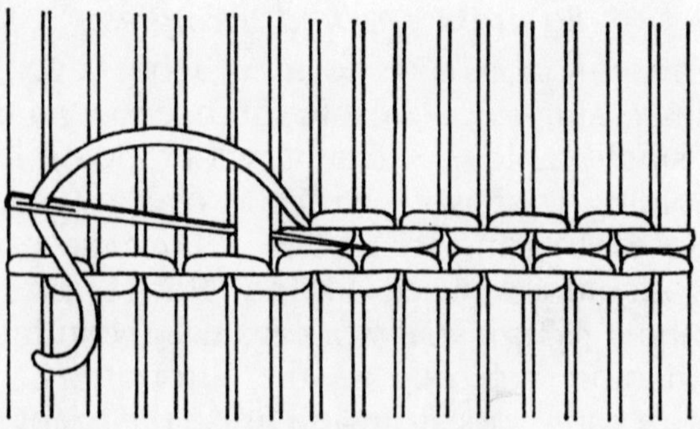

Two rows of cable stitch

Cable stitch

This stitch is worked from left to right. You should bring your needle out on the left side of the first pleat you intend to use. It is important to keep your needle parallel with the gathering threads as you stitch or you will have a row of cable that is crooked. A row of cable stitch actually consists of two rows of stitching, one top cable and one lower cable. They alternate and form naturally as you stitch. A lower cable is stitched with the thread below the needle, and the upper cable is stitched with the thread above the needle (see illustrations). Knot the end of two strands of thread prior to stitching.

How to make cable stitch

Bring your needle out (1) and take your first stitch with the thread below the needle (2). Throw the thread to the top and, keeping your needle at right angles to the pleats and maintaining a straight line across the work, take an upper cable stitch (3) and (4). Use your thumbnail to guide the stitches, if necessary, to sit close to each other, thus preventing too much fabric showing through the stitches. Mistakes are most likely to occur if you forget to change the position of the thread with each stitch. Be consistent with the depth of pleat you pick up on your needle each time — ideally about two-thirds — and work with slightly looser tension than usual.

To make stacked triangles

These shapes are formed from evenly decreasing rows of **cable stitch**, ending with a single cable. 1. Stitch a row of nine cables, holding your work with the overcast edge closest to you (see arrow). 2. Reverse your work and proceed to the 'third' row of cables. 3. Turn your work again and continue stitching, referring to the illustrations. 4. Turn your work again and finish the triangle. Take a small backstitch to secure your thread at the back of the work.

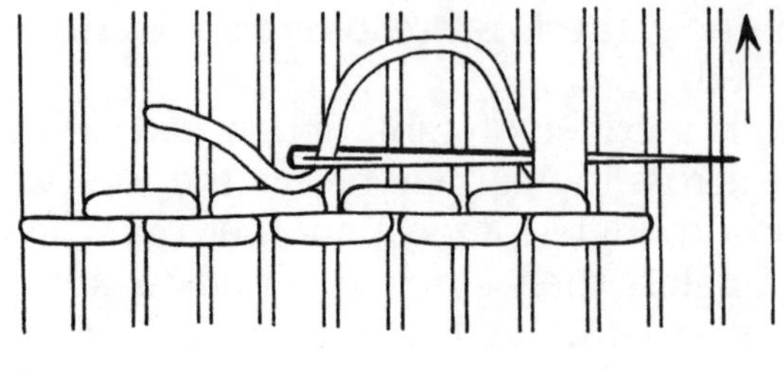

1

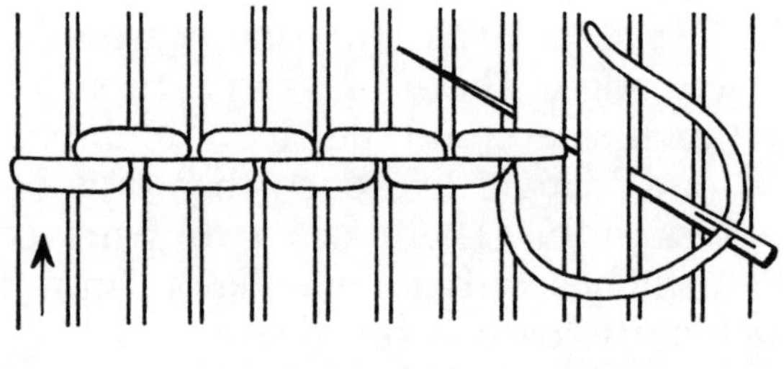

2

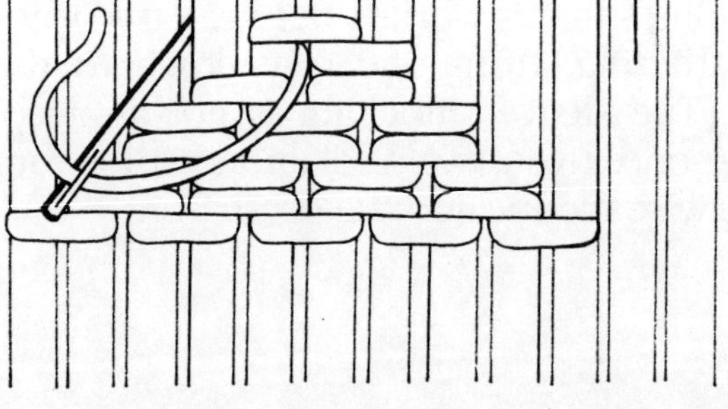

3

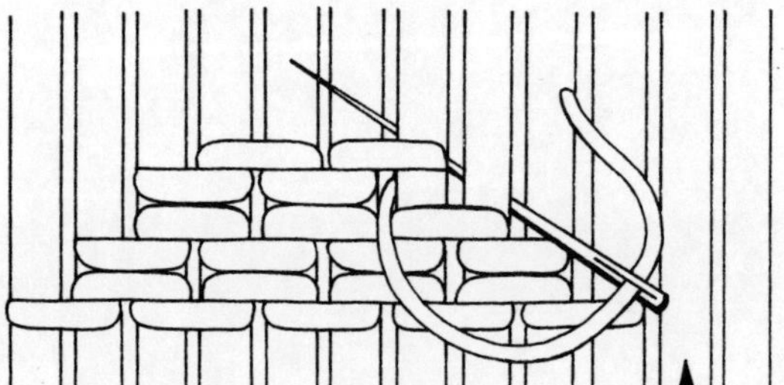

4

The four steps to creating stacked triangles

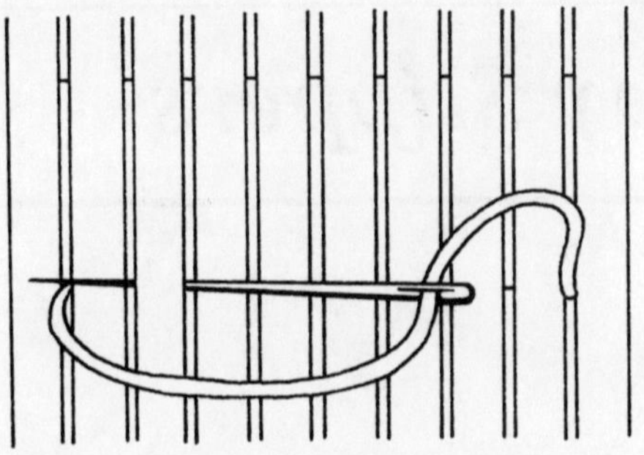

1

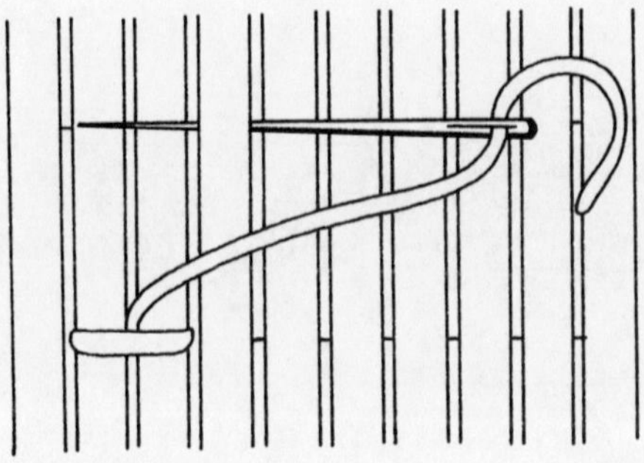

2

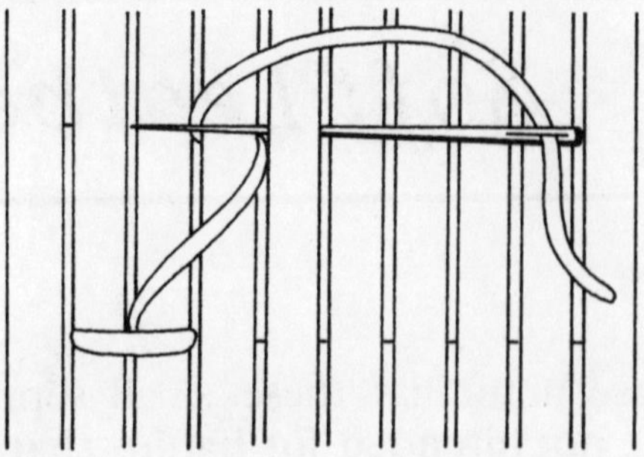

3

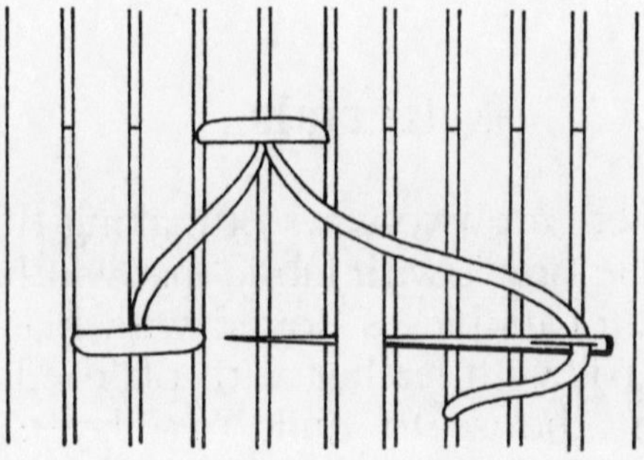

4

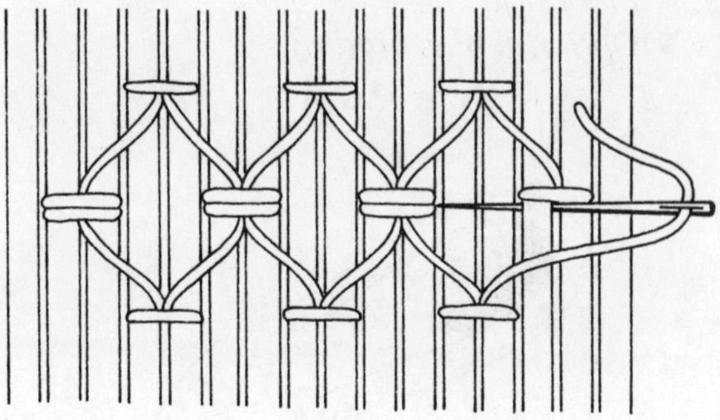

5

The five steps of diamond stitch

How to make a diamond stitch

Diamond stitch is worked using two rows of gathering stitches as guidelines. Bring your knotted two strands of thread out to the left of your first pleat. 1. Put the needle through the next pleat, keeping the needle exactly horizontal, as for cable stitch. 2. Take the next stitch level with the lower gathering thread, keeping the thread above the needle and the needle horizontal. Stitch into the next pleat. 3. With the thread below the needle, take a stitch into the adjacent pleat, as for cable stitch. 4. Keep your thread below the needle, take a stitch into the next pleat, up at the top gathering row. Keep repeating these steps until your row is finished. See the illustration for the position of the next and subsequent rows.

Soft Leather Baby Slippers

Please note that these small slippers are not intended for babies that are walking as the sole would not be thick enough and the child would slip on any smooth surface.

Materials

Note: There are two ways of making these shoes. The first is with fabric that will have the edge of its pieces bound with bias — the other is with leather, with plain edges. You may choose to quilt two layers of chamois together to create a thicker fabric.

- *Piece of soft leather, or a chamois used for cleaning cars, or quilted or thick fabric*
- *Sewing thread*
- *Ribbon for ties*
- *Optional bias binding*

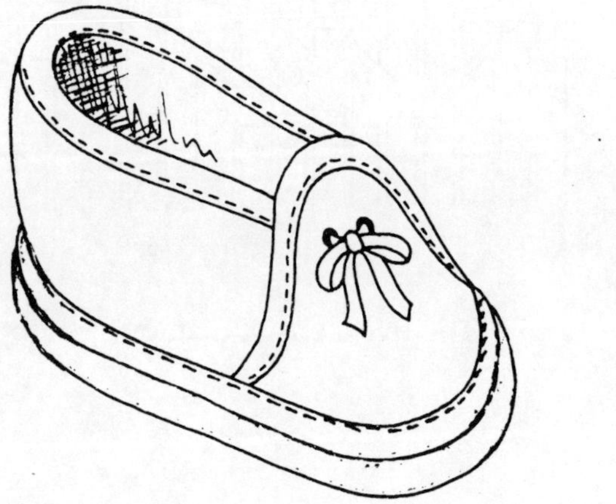

Method

Trace off the pattern onto paper. Place pattern on leather or fabric and cut out two each of soles, back/sides and front pieces for each pair of slippers. Taking care not to stretch the pieces, zig-zag over the upper edge of each back/side piece and each front piece, or bind with bias binding.

Leather shoe: Place the back/side piece, wrong sides facing, onto the sole matching the centre back positions. Zig-zag around the sole, securing the edges together. Place the front piece onto the sole, matching the centre front position, and zig-zag over these edges. Note that the back/side piece and the front piece will overlap at the sides.

Fabric shoe: Bind the edges of the two sole pieces together, running bias off as shown at centre back. Bind the edges of the upper piece in the same way. Tucking the bias ends to the inside, hand sew the two bound edges together with tiny stitches.

Punch holes through at markings and thread ribbon through to fasten the shoe.

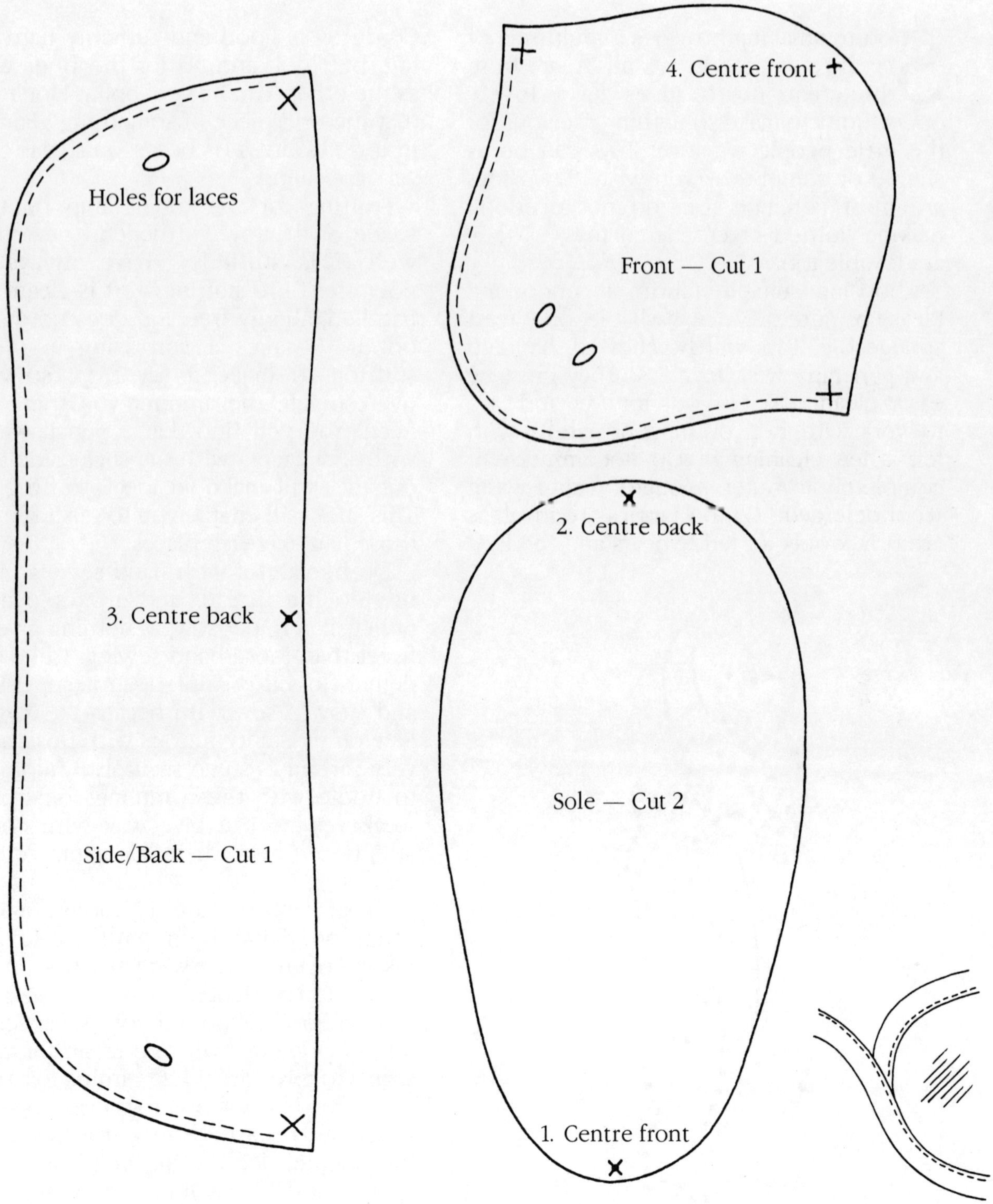
4. Centre front
Front — Cut 1
Holes for laces
3. Centre back
Side/Back — Cut 1
2. Centre back
Sole — Cut 2
1. Centre front

Soft-toy Making

Soft-toy making provides a multitude of creative outlets for us all. Apart from the creativity, it gives us a lovely opportunity to make something precious for the little people we love. Toys can be as simple or complex as you wish. Sewn toys are most common, but do not overlook making knitted or crocheted toys, as they are lovable too.

Choosing suitable fabrics is important. Please be sure they are washable, or at least spongeable. Toys will be chewed, handled and generally well 'loved' so they must be easily cleaned. Felt is good for toys, and easy to work with, but you must be careful with felt when cleaning it. Do not immerse it completely in water; sponge it using warm wool detergent. Cotton fabrics are ideal, as are firm wools for teddy bears and the like.

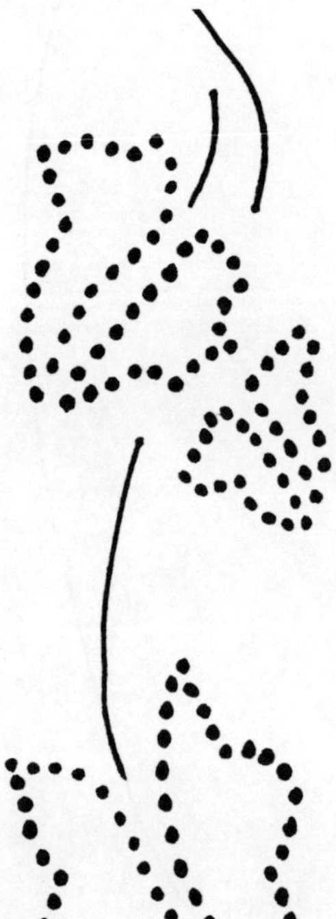

Corduroy is good and certainly hard wearing, but look around for the finer weaves as the others can be very bulky. Don't forget that the odd piece of something glamorous in a doll's dress or bear's waistcoat can be very appealing.

Stuffing for the toy is important. The shape of the toy will depend on just how well it is stuffed. I have always used polyester fibre stuffing — it is clean, easily handled, allergy free and does not have an odour. It takes a surprising amount of stuffing to make a toy firm, so always overestimate the amount you think you'll need. You will find that a pencil wrapped with sticky tape, with the sticky side on the outside, will make an ideal 'stuffing stick'. This stick will enable you to push fibre into those hard-to-reach places.

Do be careful with hand sewing. Always use double thread, and always over-sew, rather than under-sew, as nothing gives way faster than loose hand sewing. I like to use dental floss if possible as it is super-strong and easy to sew with because it is waxed. Sew on eyes and buttons with floss, and be very careful to stitch securely. Children like to fiddle with the trimmings on toys and weak sewing can give way with constant attention. Check these elements often for repairs.

Facial features are important and can often be painted on with fabric paints instead of embroidery. Practise first on paper to get just the right expression.

Stitch double around points, especially if lots of pressure will be put on them. Clip seams to give ease when turning to the right side. Pressing of fabric toys prior to stuffing is generally not necessary. It is best to have the opening for stuffing in an unobtrusive spot. If possible, avoid having it on a curve.

Stencilled Quilt

This simple idea will produce a charming, unique quilt for your home. I suggest you stencil on squares of cream pure cotton quilter's muslin (sometimes known as homespun) and it's a good idea to consider your paint and fabric colours carefully to be sure they coordinate. Choose only cotton fabric for your contrast fabric, and be sure to saturate this and your muslin squares in lukewarm water to preshrink them and remove any chemical dressing in the fabric. After drying, steam iron to smooth them.

Materials

- *16 x 30 cm (6¼" x 12") squares of prewashed quilter's muslin, plus any practice fabric needed for stencilling*
- *20 strips of contrast fabric, 30 cm long x 8 cm wide (12" x 3"), for piecing together the stencilled blocks into vertical strips*
- *5 strips of contrast fabric, 160 cm long x 8 cm wide (63" x 3"), for joining the block strips vertically, and to edge the sides*
- *4 strips of contrast fabric, 160 cm long x 5 cm wide (63" x 2"), for the binding on the sides, top and bottom edges of the quilt*
- *One piece of fabric (or lengths of fabric joined to create a piece this size) for the quilt back and one piece of quilter's batting, each 160 cm (63") square*
- *Medium-sized safety pins or long quilter's pins*
- *Sewing thread the colour of your finished stencils*
- *Acrylic paints (be sure they are suitable for application to fabric, ie they have a fabric medium included in their mixture. If not, purchase fabric medium separately and mix this with your paints)*
- *Small sea sponge for applying the paints*
- *Flat container for paint, paper kitchen towel and masking tape to hold stencils in place*

Note: The given length of the contrast strips is actually in excess of your needs, but it does allow for inevitable fabric movement during sewing and quilting. Cut away excess from ends only when you need to.

LAYOUT FOR QUILT

To stencil

If you haven't stencilled before, practise first on scrap fabric

Observe the illustration of the motif layout suggestion and decide if this pleases you. If not, rearrange the motifs to whichever combination you wish, noting how many of each you will have to stencil. Wet your brush or sponge and dry off as much moisture as possible from them. Working on a waterproof, flat surface, tape the stencil to the centre of the fabric square. Place a small amount of your paint in the container and spread out slightly. Dab your sponge down into the paint, dab off any excess onto kitchen towel, then commence dabbing paint onto the stencil spaces. Continue to do this until all the stencil is filled in. Do not strive for an overall opaque finish as stencils are meant to be slightly stippled in appearance and uneven in their colour density. **Too much paint or moisture in your sponge will create uneven stencil edges.** If you wish, use blocks as a border stencil in the corner of each square, as shown in the photograph. Set finished stencils aside to dry, then iron them on the wrong side to heat seal the paint. You are now ready to join the squares together!

Border Motif

Motif for Quilt

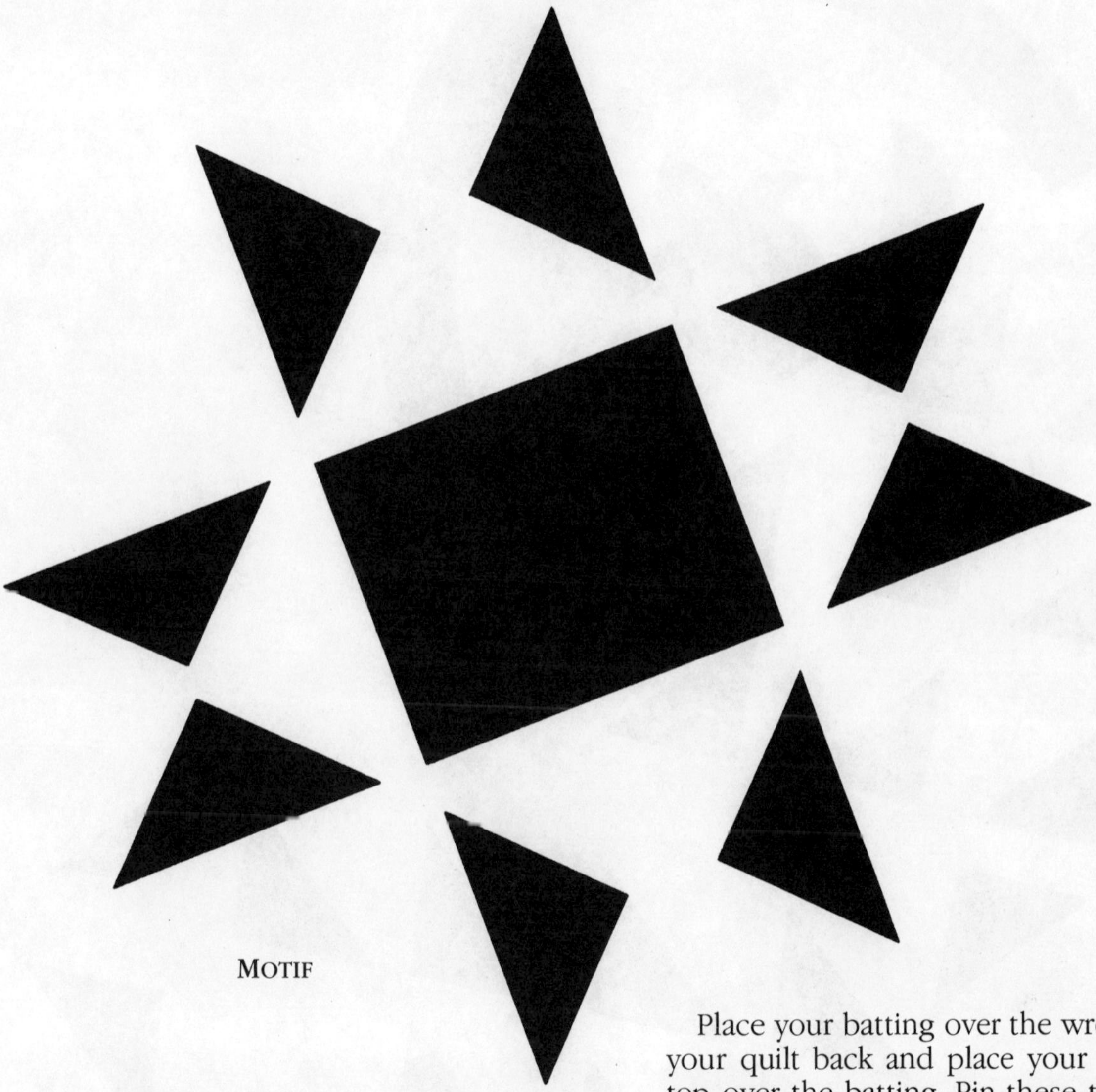

Motif

To make the quilt

If you rearranged your quilt motifs, make your own illustration to act as a guide to joining the squares in strips. Join the squares into vertical strips with a contrast strip between each, and one on each end. Use a uniform 6 mm (¼″) or 9 mm (⅜″) seam allowance throughout. You will have four vertical strips of joined squares. Join these stencilled strips with three of the five 8 cm-wide contrast strips, then sew the remaining two down each side, sewing over the ends of the short contrast strips.

Place your batting over the wrong side of your quilt back and place your sewn quilt top over the batting. Pin these three layers together, placing a pin at every sewn intersection. and elsewhere if you have sufficient pins, starting in the centre of the quilt and working outwards. Hand or machine quilt around each motif. Trim outer edges of quilt to be even with quilt top.

Place 5 cm-wide contrast strips down each side, right sides facing and raw edges matching. Taking a 1 cm seam, stitch through all thicknesses. Trim ends to be level with quilt top. Turn the binding to the wrong side, turn in 1 cm and hand hem the binding to the quilt back. Repeat this step at the top and bottom edges, taking the binding over the previously sewn edges and allowing a 1 cm allowance at each end for turning in.

MOTIF

MOTIF

Stiffened Fabric Ideas

This craft is one of the quickest creative activities I know of. Before you know it, you will have lovely bows and fabric cut-outs trimming the most basic of pots and baskets, transforming them into real decorator items. The techniques are the same for just about any fabric you may wish to stiffen, and the fabric découpage is really as simple as pasting fabric cut-outs into position, then coating them with another layer of glue! The instructions give you a choice between fabric stiffening solution, such as Boyles, or PVA glue. I find them both satisfactory, and you can even use the Jo Sonja Satin Polymer Finishing Varnish which I paint onto the fabric, rather than squeeze through. So read on, and you'll soon have some pretty and useful items to add to your home. Please note, that in the Method instructions I refer to the stiffening solutions as 'glue'.

Materials

- *Cotton fabrics of various sizes and designs*
- *Fabric stiffener solution (I suggest products made in Australia) or PVA glue, or varnish as discussed above*
- *Scissors*
- *Plastic kitchen wrap, or aluminium foil*

Method

To sew a fabric strip to use as a bow

Tie your tape measure around the pot and into a bow to check how long the bow strip has to be. If you are going to glue a bow to a basket or pot, just tie your tape measure into a bow and check its proportions against the size of the pot or basket, adjusting the size of the bow as necessary. Cut your strip of fabric twice the desired width, plus seam allowances, by the desired length. Fold the fabric over double with right sides facing and cut the ends at an angle. Stitch around the raw edges, leaving a gap in the centre for turning. Turn the tie out through the opening and press, being sure the seam edge is neat and even. Close the opening with hand sewing.

How to cut out and apply motifs for fabric découpage

Using very small sharp scissors — either embroidery or nail scissors are good — cut around the printed motif you've selected. If you don't manage to cut away all the background colour, you could paint your object the same colour as the background and the fabric background will become almost invisible. Take your time cutting out the motifs. The more care you take with accuracy, the better your trimmed object will look. You should avoid cutting too many motifs that will result in very narrow connecting strips of fabric — these are usually fairly easy to work with, but can be weakened by glue and movement. Lay completed motifs flat until they are to be used. Lay out the motifs to decide on a pleasing arrangement then, using a brush, coat the area they are to be glued to with glue, lay on the motif, then coat the motif with another layer of glue. Overlap motifs as necessary. Finish off the motifs with another coat of glue when the first coat is dry.

How to cover a frame or box with fabric

If your frame is old and painted, sand it slightly to give some roughness for the glue to adhere to. Boxes are best covered in sections, that is, each side receives its own panel, cut to overlap its neighbour slightly. Frames are covered with strips for each side that fold over to the back of the frame, with the corners cut at an angle. These angles can be tricky, but it's probably easier if you do the two side strips first, allowing the fabric to cover the mitring line slightly. Cut the fabric for the two remaining strips, making sure the mitring angles on these are precise (they will overlap the first strips slightly). This way no part of the frame shows through at the angle.

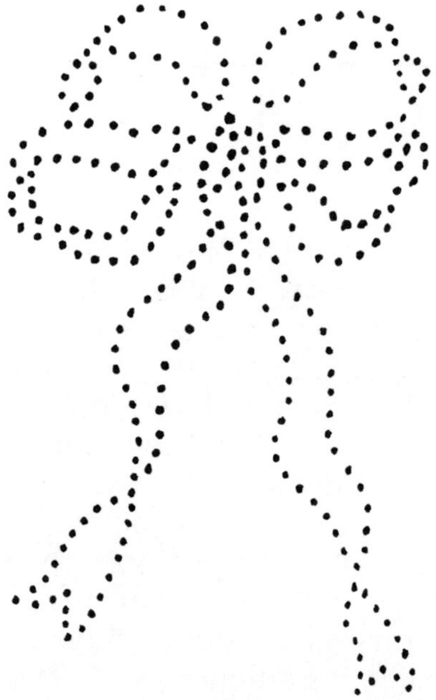

To fasten strips or panels of fabric to boxes or frames, coat the box or frame surface about to be covered with glue, lay on the fabric and smooth it into place. Cover the fabric with another layer of glue and use your brush or fingers to smooth out any wrinkles. Cut fabric at necessary angles to allow for overlaps or joins, or to remove fullness. Check the object during the drying period to be sure nothing has moved, and adjust if necessary. If disaster strikes in some way, that is, something moves or wrinkles, dampen the area with a little water to soften and adjust as best you can. This glue will dry crystal clear and give the surface a slight sheen.

How to stiffen a bow

Note the instructions illustrated on page 98 for tying the bows — one method will achieve a bow that is tied, then glued into place, the other method shows how to tie a fabric strip around a pot, or similar, and then tie the bow with the tails of the strip. Make your fabric strip as instructed above. *Here comes the messy bit!* Thoroughly immerse and saturate the strip with glue. Working quickly, once the strip is thoroughly wet with glue, tie your bow, or your strip, around your pot or basket and then into a bow. Scrunch up wads of kitchen plastic wrap and tuck these inside the loops of the bow to hold their shape. Lay the bow onto a surface covered with plastic wrap and adjust the tails, tucking more plastic wrap under and among these to hold the desired shape. If you are placing a bow at the top of a frame, hold the bow to decide just where the tails should loop to, and adjust as necessary. You will be best able to make further adjustments as the bow dries slightly. If it is not yet dry and totally wrong, or you change your mind, spray it with water and readjust the bow. Any bits of fabric that appear to be less glue-covered than others, can be coated with more glue using the brush, as the drying process continues.

How to make pot-pourri sacks

Cut two oblong-shaped fabric pieces (approx 35 x 25 cm, 13¾″ x 10″) and round off the lower corners. Place the two pieces together and, with right sides facing, stitch around the curved sides of the sacks. Turn to the right side and tuck the top 10 cm (4″) down into the sack. Stitch it in place at the raw edge. Make your fabric strip as described earlier. Read the preceeding paragraph for fabric stiffening method, being sure the sacks are thoroughly saturated with glue. Fill the sack base with plastic wrap wads, and tie the glue-saturated fabric strip around the sack, tightening it and tying a bow, but still allowing for a hole at the top through which you will insert pot-pourri. Adjust the neck of the sack attractively so that it fans out above the bow. Support this with more plastic wrap if necessary. The sack should now look plump, have a flat bottom, a narrow neck, and a 'frilled' top, with a pretty tie and bow sitting just below the top. Sit it flat and allow it to dry thoroughly, adjusting it as necessary while the drying process continues, making sure it will sit flat when completely dry. Fill each with pot-pourri and enjoy the perfume!

PS. A gentle blast with the hair dryer will often speed up slow drying areas, and any area that dries less stiff than others can be painted with more glue and allowed to dry. Remember, the more glue you apply, the stiffer the object becomes.

Sweet Hearts for Children's Parties

Cut two of this simple shape from cardboard, weave them together as shown and, before you know it, a pretty heart appears ready to be filled with goodies to take home. The first time you attempt this project may be a little frustrating for you, so — take my advice and have a cup of tea ready, and don't lose your sense of humour!

1. Starting off the first row.
2. Next step of second row.
3. The first row is finished.
4. Starting off the second row.
5. Weaving the second row.
6. The second row is finished. Repeat the first and second rows to complete weaving. Cut a strip of cardboard 25 cm x 1.5 cm (10″ x ⅝″) for the handle and glue, or staple its ends at opposite 'dips' inside in the basket rim.

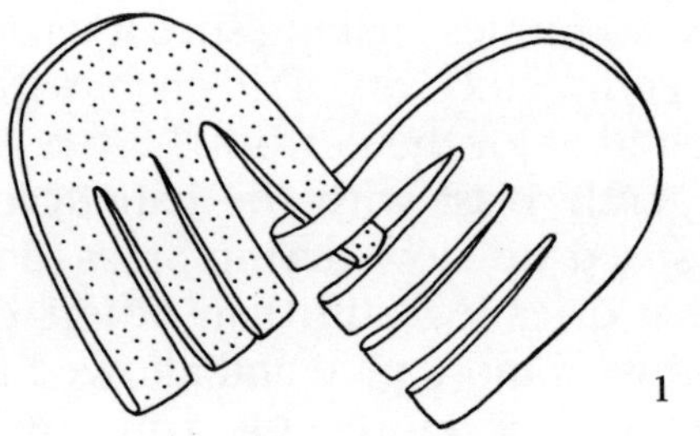

1

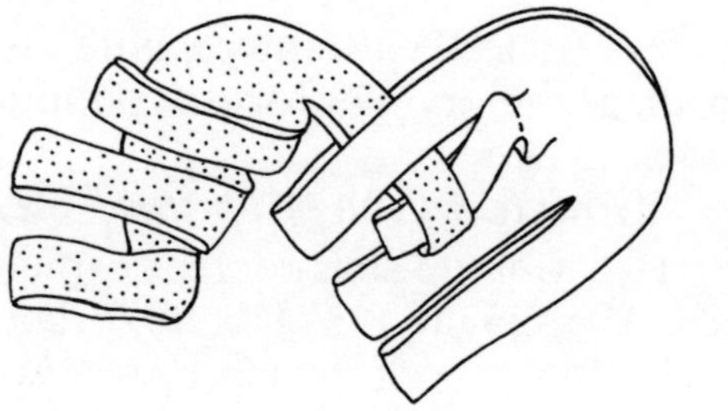

2

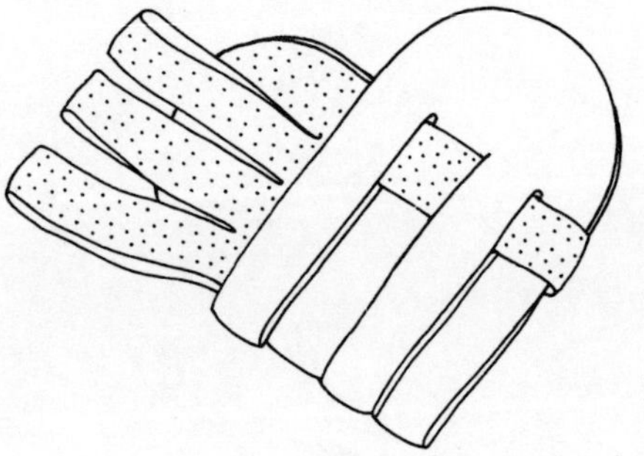

3

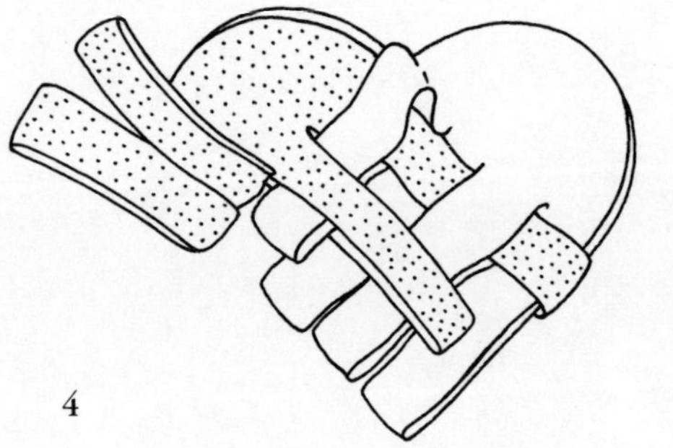

4

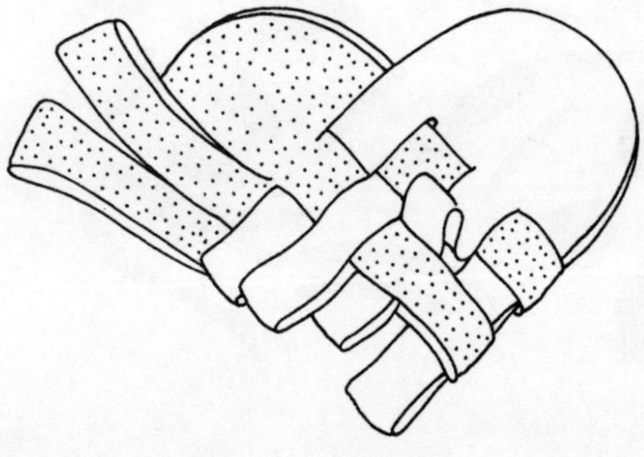

5

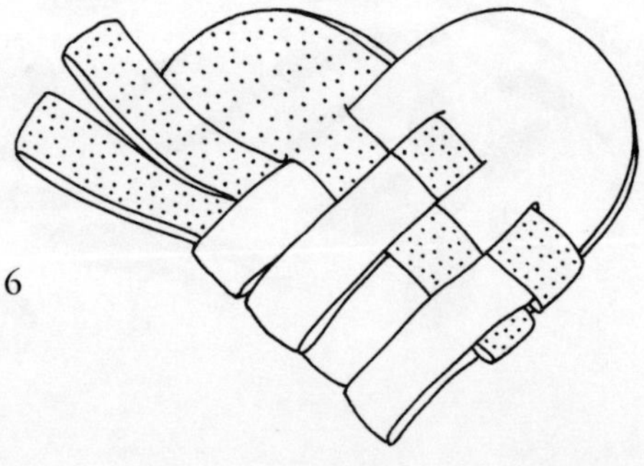

6

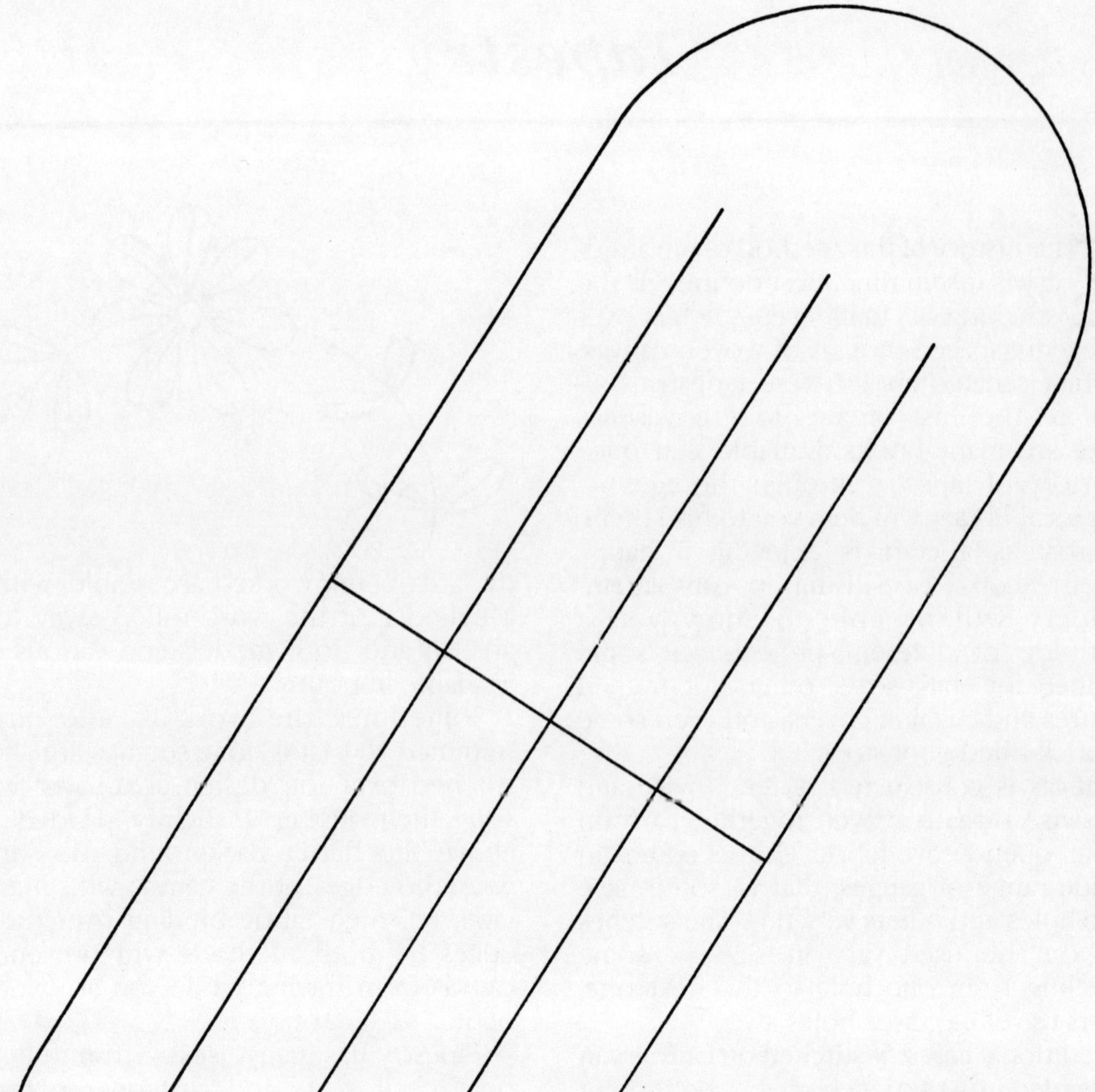

BASIC SHAPE FOR SWEET HEARTS

Tapestry

The history of this method of embroidery is lost in time. Best defined as the stitching of small, even stitches over the evenly spaced threads of woven canvas, the first ornate 'fabrics' were tapestries — as were the first ornate floor coverings. There are many books available that trace the story of tapestry through the ages — your local library will help you to find them. Tapestry as a craft is enjoying a happy revival. Shops specialising in canvas embroidery will be able to show you a multitude of different projects — some destined for chair seats, others for framed pictures and cushion covers, and even some for brick-filled door stops.

Canvas is constructed of lengthwise and crosswise threads woven together to form a firm, open-weave fabric. Canvas comes in a wide range of gauges, that is, some have large holes and others very tiny. The stitches that can be used vary in size — some travelling from one hole to the next one, others travelling three holes away.

Traditional tapestry stitched on canvas can be divided into two categories — petit point and gros point. The difference here is simply the size of the spaces in the canvas. Petit point is worked on very fine canvas and requires a finer needle and thread. Gros point is the opposite, being worked on larger canvas, using thicker wools and needles. Petit point, naturally, takes much longer to finish than gros point, and you will usually find smaller pieces in petit point. Sometimes the two techniques are combined on petit point canvas — gros point being worked over several of the smaller squares to give the larger stitches.

Working frames are important when stitching tapestry. They help to keep the canvas neat and undistorted. They can keep

the area being worked accessable, with the remainder of the work rolled away. There are lap and floor models and various sizes available in both.

Sometimes the work is sold already trammed — that is, long stitches are already stitched over the design area, over which you stitch, giving a slightly padded look above the flatter background. Be sure to wrap the edges of the canvas with masking tape, or stitch fabric binding over the raw edges — both methods will prevent the canvas from fraying while you are working on it.

Tapestry has many uses — from full-sized rugs, chair seats and cushions, to framed pictures and book covers. Let your imagination run riot with ideas on how to use your finished work.

Professional framers will neaten the finished piece and stretch it into place prior to framing the work — or using it on a chair, or for a similar purpose.

If you are starting a tapestry for the first time, there are many, many books available on the subject, some just right for the beginner. There are many specialist shops that will give you all sorts of good advice about getting started, the equipment needed and the level of projects to take on.

I must warn you, though, to be careful; it's addictive!

Tie-on Director's Chair Cover

You don't need a pattern to cover and transform that old director's chair. It's a breeze if you follow these simple instructions. This cover is simply one large piece of fabric bunched and draped to the necessary size. You will have to join fabric lengths to achieve the correct dimensions, or you could use a large bed-sheet — there are plenty of great designs from which to choose, so why not?

Materials

- *Director's chair*
- *Fabric to cover chair and cushion*
- *Medium-sized piping cord for edge trim if desired*
- *Quilter's wadding for seat cushion (optional)*
- *Sewing thread*
- *String*

Method

To make chair covering:

Join lengths of your chosen fabric to make a large square. Practise on a double bed sheet to see what size square you will need. You may have to join fabric at selvedges to achieve the correct area of fabric. Wash fabric before use if you are worried it may shrink. Press seams open. Open out square and place it over chair, pressing it into corners and bundling it up around bases of arms and into seat area. Pin to secure while this fitting process is carried out. Once you are satisfied with fit and drape, mark positions of twelve buttonholes. Mark one either side of front arm bases. Mark one either side of back arm bases on inside of chair, and another one either side on the outside. You will now have four buttonholes marked around each of the back arm bases, and two at each of the front bases. Remove fabric from chair and make 3 cm (1¼″) long buttonholes as marked. Reposition fabric on chair. Tie string through buttonholes to secure. Trim around base at floor level to create an even length. Remove fabric from chair, discard string and hem lower edge as marked or fold edge over piping cord and stitch it down with the zipper foot of your machine.

Make ties from scrap fabric cut away from hem. You could face them with a pretty contrasting fabric. Cut strips for the ties about 1 m x 22 cm (39″ x 9″). Fold double lengthways with right sides facing. Sew around all edges leaving an opening for turning. Turn and press. Insert ties through buttonholes and tie into bows at base of arms and back of chair.

To make the optional frilled cushion

Cut out two pieces of fabric, the same size as chair seat plus seam allowances. For the frill, cut out two strips 22 cm (9″) wide and equal in length to twice the circumference of the seat cushion. Allow for the seams. Sew short ends of frill, press in half lengthways. Gather raw edges of frill, stitch around edge of one cushion piece. With right sides facing, stitch back to front, leaving opening. Baste several layers of wadding together to use as cushion pad. Insert pad and close opening by hand.

Tissue-box Cover

Next time you finish a box of tissues, save the box and transform it into a pretty cover for your next new box — and for all those boxes after that one!

Materials

- *Cardboard tissue box*
- *Scissors*
- *Aquadhere glue*
- *Gathered or straight lace for trimming*
- *Fine polyester wadding*
- *Fabric to cover box*
- *Ribbons for ties*

Method

Cut away the base of the tissue box, and then carefully cut up the corners, allowing the cardboard to lay flat. Glue wadding to wrong side of cover (the shiny, right side is difficult to glue), trimming it close to edges. Snip around edges in centre and wrap wadding underneath, then glue.

Cut fabric to shape of cardboard, allowing 2 cm (1″) all round. Wrap all fabric edges underneath and glue, repeating for the centre area. Make sure fabric is smooth, and not over-tight.

Fold the cover back into shape and place it over a box of tissues. It will be slightly shorter in depth, so add lace at the lower edge to equal the length of the tissue box, or a little longer. Add lace around centre if desired. Cover edge of lace with glued ribbon lengths, allowing tails of 20 cm (8″) at edges. These tails of ribbon tie into bows to hold the cover together. Add ribbon trim to centre if desired.

Tonia's Country Rabbits

These dear little rabbits would look charming joined into a pram chain. I do not suggest babies chew them — there are too many things that could be easily removed and therefore they could be unsafe.

Materials

- *Felt*
- *Fabric scraps*
- *Embroidery thread*
- *Polyester fibre stuffing*

Method

Cut two ears and two body shapes from felt, and two pants pieces — adding 6 mm (¼″) seam allowances — and fabric strips for straps from cotton fabric. Place them together in pairs with edges matching. Zig-zag around the edges — leave a space just below one arm in the rabbit for stuffing, stitching around completely. Tie a knot in the centre of the ears. Stuff the rabbit and hand sew the opening closed.

Turn over waist and leg pants edges 6 mm and stitch. Place pants pieces together with right sides facing and edges even and stitch down sides and around crotch. Turn to right side, fold over raw edges of strap strips and stitch. Attach straps at front 'X's and place pants on rabbit. Make pants fit around waist by making small pleats near straps, and hand sew around in place onto rabbit, attaching back of straps as you stitch. Embroider facial features, stitch on ears to centre of head and make embroidery floss bow around neck.

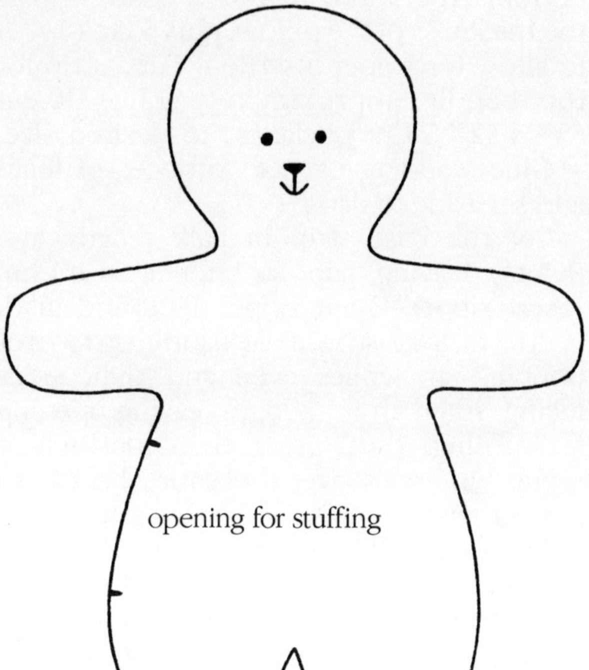

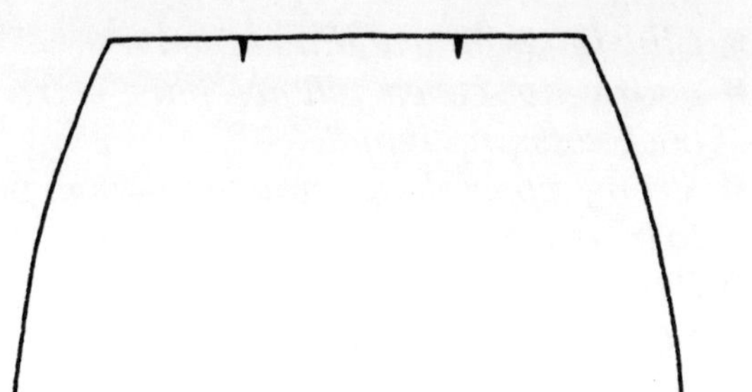

Travel Pillow

This is simply a pillow with a handle. It can be carried conveniently to the football, the opera, to where you like to go fishing, or to any place where there will be hard seating to contend with. Anyone who cannot sleep easily in an unfamiliar bed will like taking this friendly pillow along, too.

Considerations

Virtually any size of pillow can be made to this design, although it must be said that the process works best when the shape is square or rectangular. The amount of fabric you require will depend, obviously, on the pillow size.

Materials

- *Piece of foam rubber of desired pillow size*
- *Quilter's wadding to cover all surfaces of foam*
- *Glue to fasten wadding to foam*
- *Fabric to cover pillow, plus extra for pocket(s) and handle*
- *Strong zipper, long enough to allow pillow to be inserted*
- *Piping*
- *Sewing thread*

Method

Cutting notes

Add 1.5 cm (⅝″) seam allowances to all pieces. Cut two main pieces of fabric the size of the front and back. Cut a strip the length of two sides and the top. The width of this strip should be the thickness of the pillow. Cut another strip the length of the bottom. The width of this second strip is the thickness of the pillow, plus 3 cm (1¼″) to allow for zipper insertion. Cut a strip for the handle approximately 12 x 30 cm (5″ x 12″). Cut pocket(s) to desired size.

Glue wadding over all surfaces of foam and set aside to dry.

Cut the base strip in half, lengthways. Rejoin, leaving gap for zipper insertion. Insert zipper. Open zipper. Find and mark centre of long strip. Fold handle strip over double, raw edges even and right sides facing, stitch around edges leaving opening for turning. Turn, press, then topstitch at regular intervals over the entire handle to strengthen it.

Centre handle over centre mark. Stitch each handle end with an 'X' to secure. Join short ends of strips to create a circle. Mark 'Vs' in the edge of the strips where corners of front and back should be positioned. Stitch pocket(s) to front and back centres. Stitch piping around front and back, clipping into corners to ease. Stitch one side of the edge strip to front, then repeat for back, matching corner points and following previous row of stitching for piping. Use your zipper foot to make this easier. Turn out through zipper. Insert pillow.

Trimming Sandshoes

Low-cost sandshoes, happy shoes and fabric slip-ons are easy to transform with simple materials such as lace, ribbons, buttons, fabric flowers, PVA glue, fabric paints and stick-on jewels. Some decorating ideas are listed below:

- *Paint shoe sections with glue, then apply lace by pressing it down onto the glued surface, adding more glue on top if necessary, and then trimming it away where the fabric shoe section joins the rubber sections. This glue dries fairly quickly and fabric is best cut when it is partially dry. Thread lace through for shoe laces.*
- *Use tartan ribbon in much the same way as lace, adding 3 mm-wide (⅛") ribbon around the edge of the fabric part of the shoe for emphasis. Thread ribbon through for laces, adding Christmas bells to the ribbon ends — noisy but good fun for Christmas! Ribbon laces are possibly the quickest, easiest transformation you can make to any sandshoe.*
- *Using fabric paints that come in squeeze-bottles with a fine, pointed tip, mark in decorative designs, such as a continuous line similar to cornelli work (like a snail trail), hearts, circles, suns and moons — the list is endless! Make the hearts by placing two raised dots of paint side by side, then use a fine paintbrush to drag paint from the dots downwards into a point, creating a heart.*
- *Stick on jewels using special glue called Jewel-It (a PVA-based glue that remains flexible when dry — there are also Australian-made versions of this product). Paint motifs among the jewels for extra effect.*
- *Trim the ribbon shoelaces across into deep 'V's and apply Fray-stop liquid (a product which prevents fabric fraying) to the ends. You will need this for lace shoelaces, too. Cut off the ends of laces and fold the raw ends under, stitching them to the backs of satin or jewelled motifs, or glue or stitch them between two buttons.*
- *Using a laundry marking pen, collect signatures on your sandshoes to have your own 'Signature Sandshoes'. Add ribbon laces and they're good for end-of-school!*

Tying a Bow Around Something

The spots illustrate the right side of the ribbon. Please disregard this if your ribbon or fabric is the same both sides. For your guidance, the illustrations serve to show which side of the ribbon or fabric is where, at what time during the bow tying process. If your ribbon or fabric has a right and a wrong side, twist it to have the right side facing you before you make step 5.

1. Bring the left-hand strand down over the right-hand strand and under. Tighten both strands.
2. Make a loop with the left-hand strand.
3. Holding the left loop, bring the right strand down over your fingers.
4. Begin to push the right strand up so that it passes between your fingers holding the left loop and the original tie made in Step 1.
5. Continue pushing the right strand through to make a full loop.
6. Tighten the bow by pulling on both loops until they sit evenly.

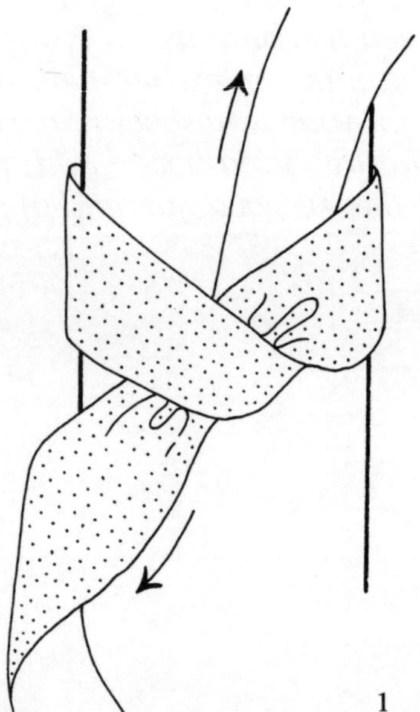

1

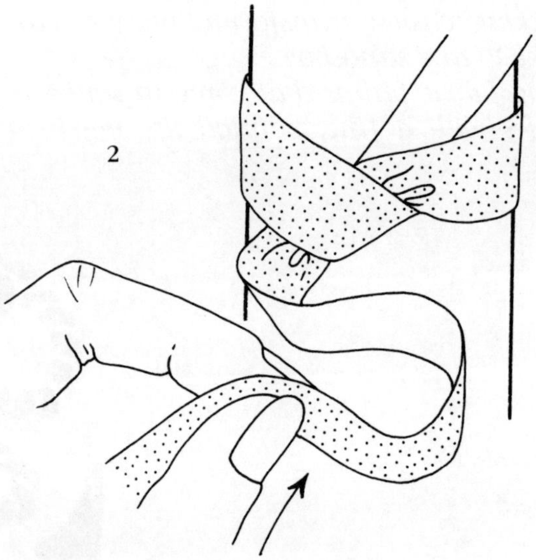

2

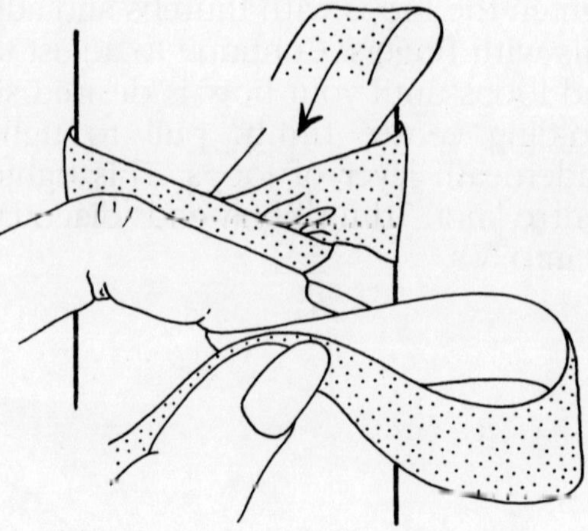

3

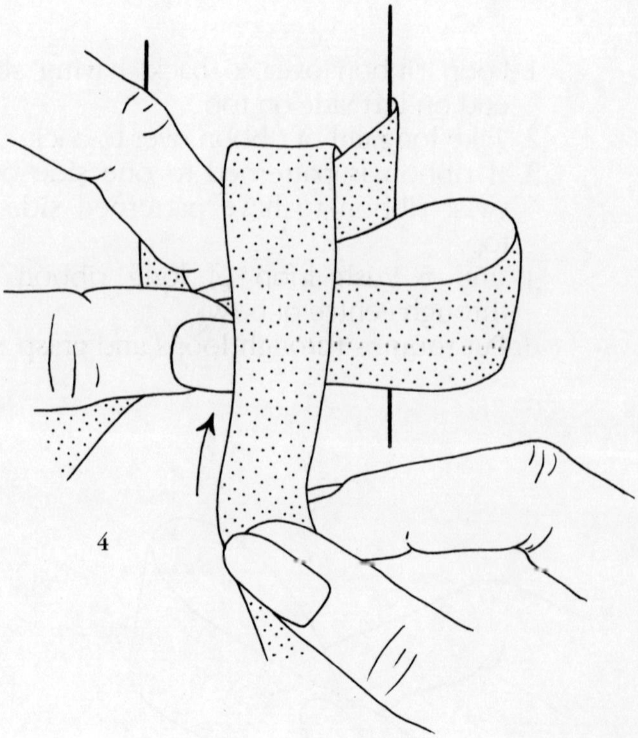

4

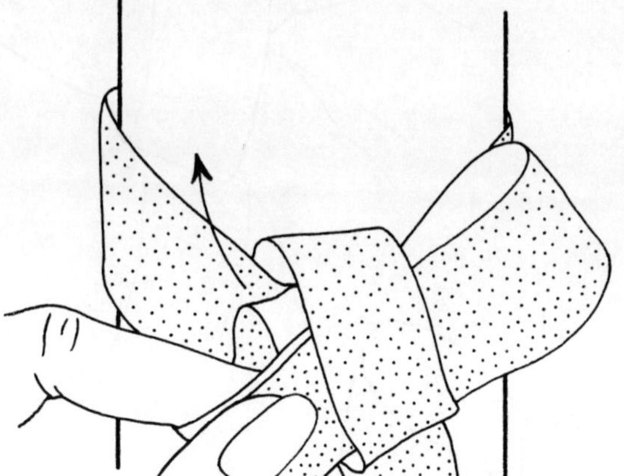

5

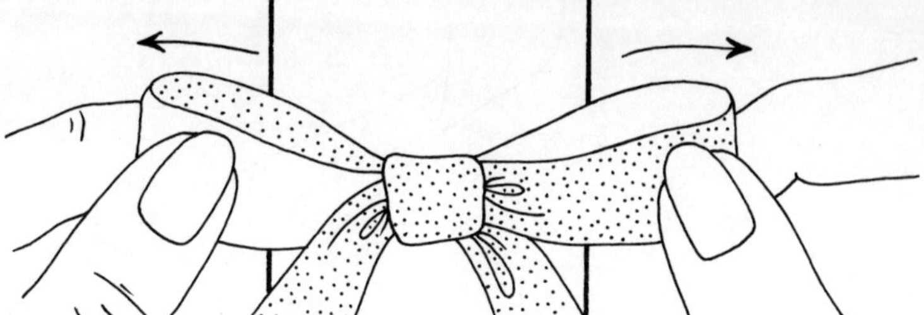

6

Tying a Bow to Fasten onto Something

1. Loop ribbon over to back, having short end on left side on top.
2. Take long tail of ribbon over to back.
3. If ribbon is patterned to one side only, twist ribbon to have patterned side on top.

4 and 5. Push loop of long ribbon tail through centre of bow.

6. Put thumbs through loops and grasp tails between little finger and ring fingers. After some practice, you will be able to tighten the loops with thumbs and adjust tails with fingers. Continue to adjust tails and loops until your bow is desired size.
7. Holding centre firmly, pull to tighten underneath layer of loops. This tightens centre knot. Trim ribbon ends diagonally, or into 'V's.

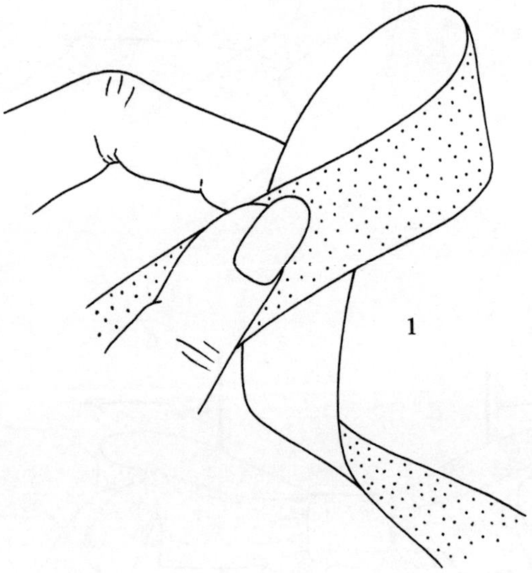

1

2

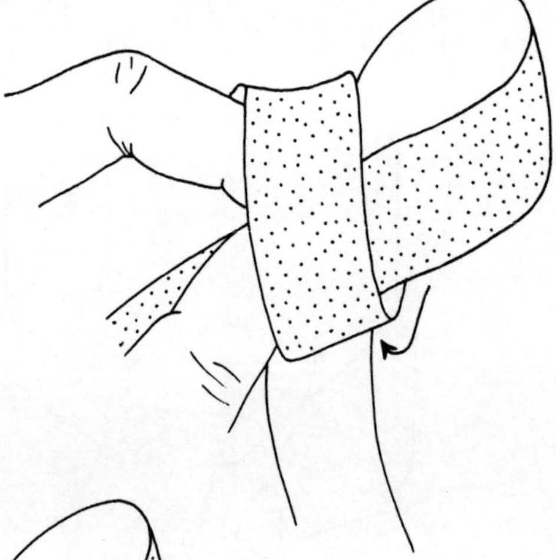

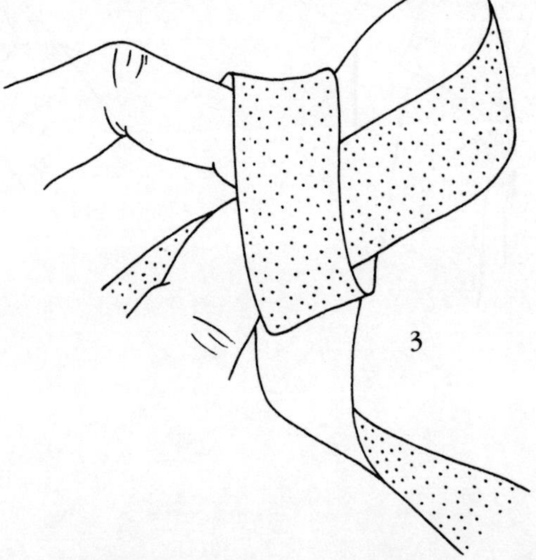

3

4

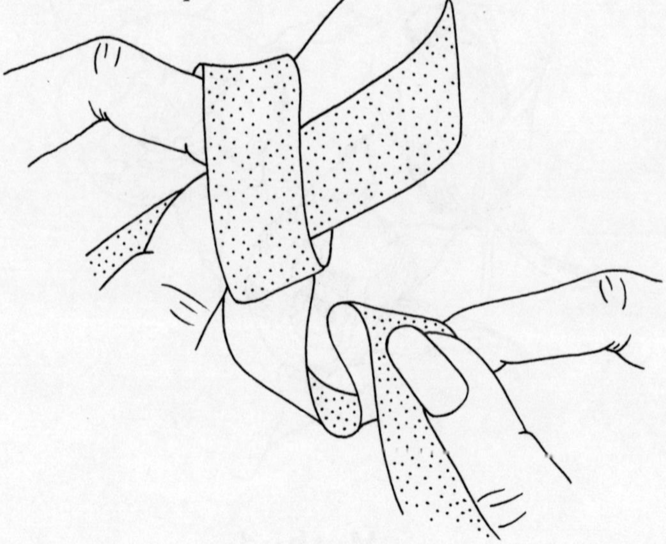

5

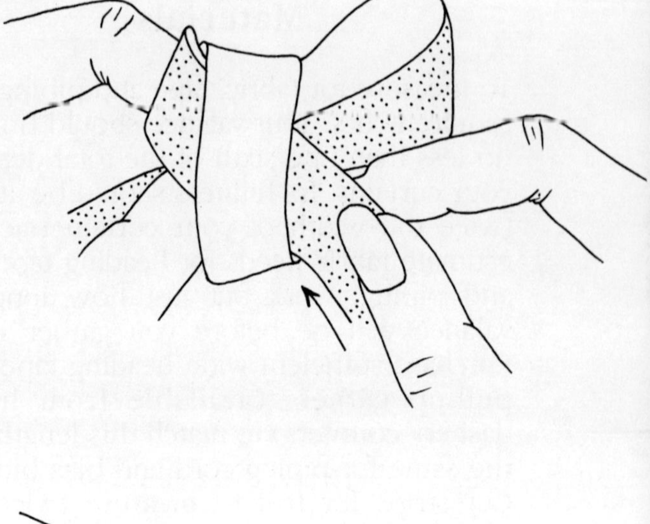

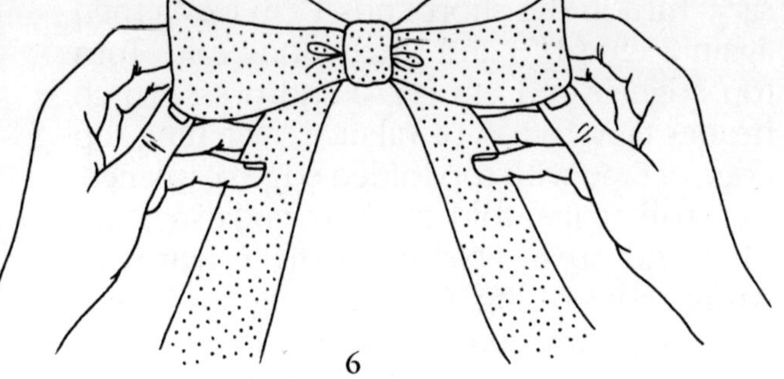

6

7

Valance or Gathered Pelmet

This curtain treatment is quite unashamedly country-style and is timeless in its appeal. It's surprisingly easy to make. If you hang a gathered valance so that the lower edge just covers the headings on your curtains, it can give the impression that your windows are taller than they actually are. I've added a frill to the lower edge to complete the look, with bias piping between the valance and the frill trim. Take into account any pattern matching needed when purchasing your fabric.

Materials

To measure for fabric, tape and piping cord requirements: Your valance should finish at no less than one sixth of the total depth of your curtains. Its fullness should be at least twice the width of your curtain track. To estimate fabric needs for heading tape, frill and piping, work out just how long the valance will be before you gather it up. Purchase sufficient wide heading tape with pull-up gathers (available from haberdashery counters) to match this length, and the same for piping cord and bias binding. Cut strips for frill to measure twice this length, plus 4 cm (2″).

Method

Cut your fabric into widths of the required valance depth and join at the selvedges, matching the printed pattern where necessary. Turn in the short ends 1 cm (½″) then again 2 cm (1″) and stitch along fold. Turn top edge over 1 cm (½″) and press. Stitch header tape to top of valance, matching top edge of tape with top folded edge of valance. Join frill strips, fold in short ends by 2 cm (1″) and press. Fold frill strip in half with wrong sides facing. Gather along raw edges. Enclose piping cord inside bias binding and stitch to make piping. Pin and stitch piping along right side and raw edge of valance, raw edges matching.

Pin gathered frill along piped edge, right sides facing and raw edges matching. Stitch through all thicknesses following previous row of stitching. Draw up gathering cords in header tape and adjust to correct length. Insert curtain hooks and hang valance.

Vera the Virtuous Vine Tamer

Materials

- *2 small bundles of raffia*
- *Scissors*
- *Fabric, approximately 30 cm x 15 cm (12″ x 6″)*

Method

From a small bundle of raffia, cut away the coarse ends and halve the bundle. Then reverse one half and replace it against the other half so that the cut ends are at both ends. Tie a raffia strand around the middle and trim the knot ends.

Cut away the coarse ends of another small raffia bundle and tie a bow around the bundle about 25 cm (10″) from the cut end. Fold the short ends down at the bow and tuck the tied piece from step 1 between the two ends of raffia, so that the short ends sit below where piece 1 crosses. Holding the layers together, tie a raffia strand around the layers, binding them and being sure to have caught all the short pieces at the back. Tie a knot in the strand and cut away the ends.

Cut a fabric piece, approximately 30 cm x 15 cm (12″x 6″), fold it over double and cut a finger-length split down through the middle. Open out the split and place it over Vera's head. Tie a raffia strand around her waist and into a bow at the front.

Hang her by her head bow in the garden shed and extract raffia strands to tame your roses, beans, creepers or whatever! These are terrific fete sellers!

Wheat Heart

So much wheat and grain comes with the lovely stems attached, and this project will produce some very pretty country-style ornaments. The size of the heart is up to you — the longer and thicker your wheat stems, the bigger your heart will finish. Tartan ribbon looks most effective tied around the stems. You only require a few strands of raffia for tying wheat, or some other grain with stems attached, and some ribbon for trim.

1. Soak the stems of a bunch of wheat (about 20 strands) in a bucket of warm water for about 20 minutes to soften. Do not wet the heads. Dry off with a towel. Tie the strands together just below the heads with some raffia.
2. Tie the strands again about 10 cm (4″) up from the first tie.
3. Divide the strands into halves and plait them, tying off the ends to secure.
4. Bring the ends of the plaits around in a heart shape and sit them behind the first tie, tying them all together to secure.
5. Add a hanging loop at the second tie, if required, and tie a bow around the first tie.

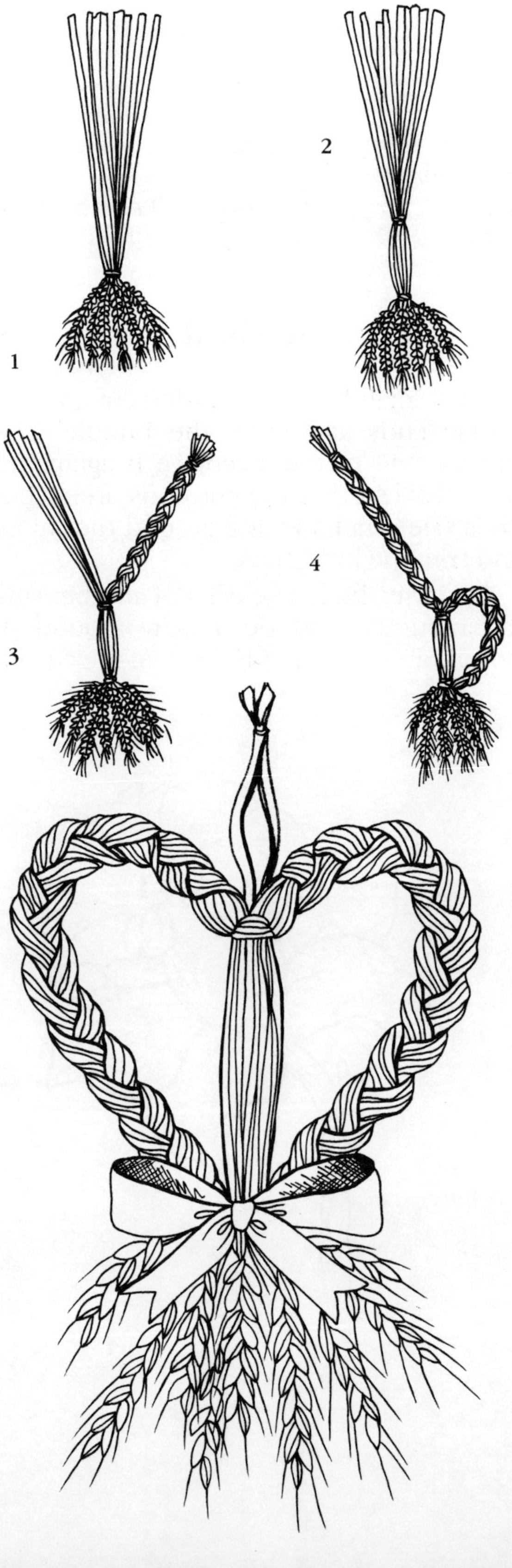

Wired Roses and Rose Buds

These simple roses make good trims for all sorts of places. With a little practice you'll soon be making whole posies of them. For each rose, you need about 35 cm (14″) of 38 mm-wide (1½″) satin or cut-edge ribbon, some florist's wire and some florist's stem tape and some thin binding wire, such as fuse wire. For each bud you'll need squares of 57 mm-wide (2¼″) satin ribbon, plus wires and stem tape. The spotted surfaces in the illustrations represent the right side of the ribbon. These ribbon techniques are courtesy of Offray Ribbons.

Roses

1. Begin by winding the fuse wire round the stem wire about 25 mm (1″) from the tip and winding upwards. Then fold the tip of the stem wire over about 12 mm (½″) and wind the fuse wire round to secure it.
2. Hold the end of the piece of ribbon so that the cut edge is horizontal. Lay the hook against the left-hand edge of the ribbon and wind the cut edge of the ribbon tightly onto the hook. Secure with binding wire.

ROSES

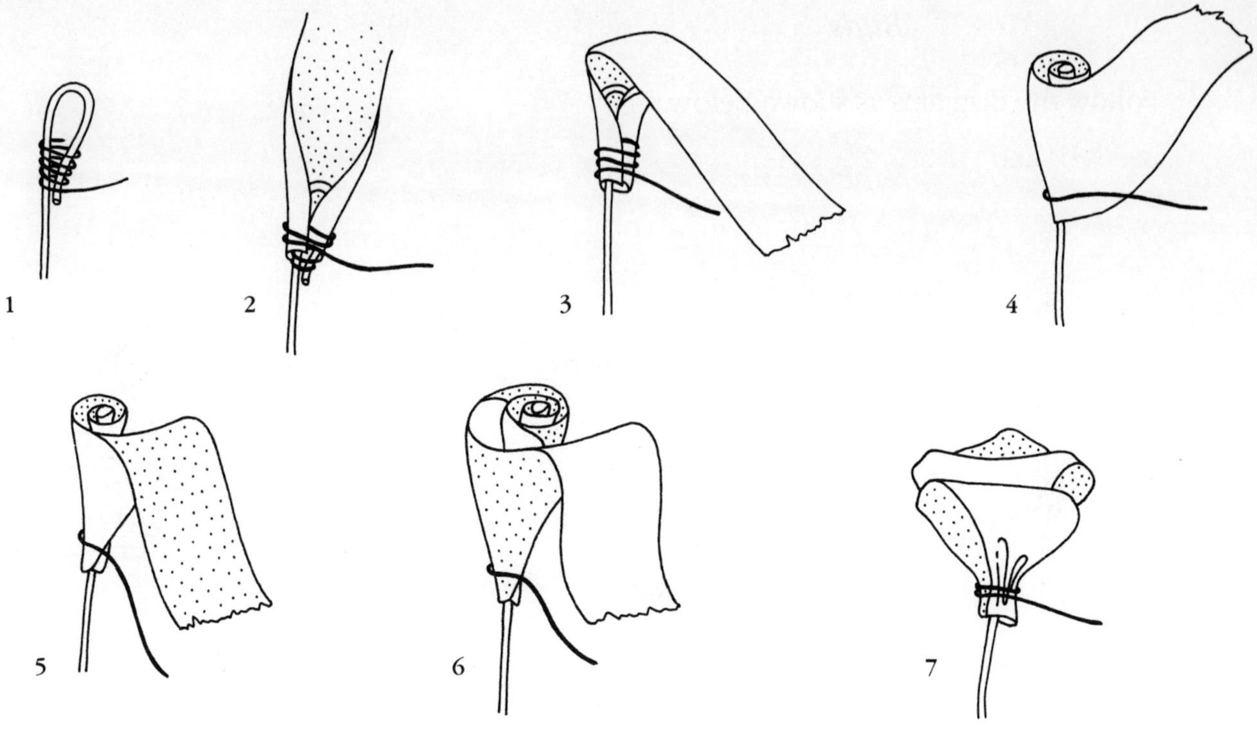

3. Now fold the length of the ribbon down over the hook tip.
4. Continue by winding the ribbon anticlockwise round the stem about three times. This covers the stem wire. Wind the binding wire round to secure the base.
5. To make the petals, hold the stem in your left (or non-working) hand. Hold the ribbon in your right (or working) hand. Make a diagonal fold towards you and, keeping the fold level with the top of the rose centre, continue to twist the stem anticlockwise.
6. When the ribbon has straightened out again, make another diagonal fold.
7. Continue making petals like this until the ribbon is used up — you'll find that the binding wire is binding the rose base as you twist the stem. Finally, gather the cut end of the ribbon at the base and bind with wire to secure. To cover the stem with stem tape, hold the end of the stem tape against the base of the rose. Twist the stem so that the tape adheres to the stem wire. If you are adding leaves, bind them in against the stem as you tape.

Buds

Follow the diagrams as shown below.

BUDS

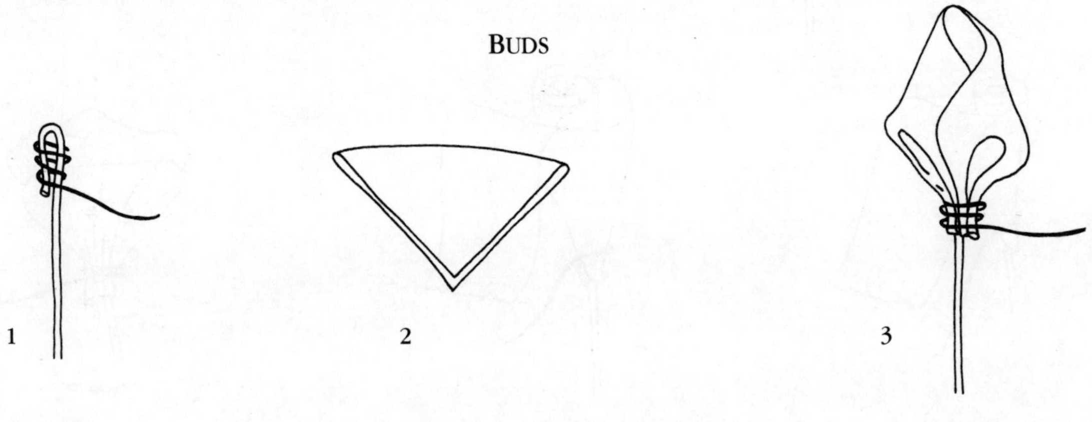

Woollen Blanket for Baby

This may not be an ideal embroidery project for beginners — though the concept could certainly become simpler for those starting out on their embroidery career! Beginners could substitute some simple stitches, such as lazy daisy, chain, stem and satin, and could use the basic design as a guide for their own ideas. Embroidering on wool is remarkably easy, and, as the blanket is backed with fabric, the underside doesn't have to be a vision of neatness! Wool blanketing is available by the metre from craft and embroidery shops, and comes in a variety of colours. I've made a traditional edging of blanket stitch using a tapestry wool yarn, though you may choose to bind the edges with satin blanket binding. This beautiful blanket was expertly worked for me by talented needlewoman and teacher, Silvia Kennedy.

Materials

- *Piece of wool blanketing, approximately 80 cm x 116 cm (32" x 46½")*
- *Piece of backing fabric (preferably lightweight cotton or wool) the same size*
- *4.20 m (5 yd 8") of satin blanket binding, or extra tapestry yarn for blanket stitch edge (check this quantity of binding against the size of your blanket, allowing for turning at corners)*
- *1 packet of tapestry chenille needles, sized 18, or similar*
- *Embroidery threads as follows — all are DMC brand:*
  Tapestry wool:
  7503 Dark yellow — 1 skein
  7745 Light yellow — 2 skeins
  7404 Green — 1 skein
  7200 Pink — 2 skeins
  7244 Lilac — 1 skein
  7302 Blue — 4 skeins
  Stranded cotton:
  224 Pink — 1 skein
  3042 Lilac — 1 skein
  3046 Lemon — 1 skein
  Ecru — 1 skein
  Medici thread:
  8799 Blue — 1 skein
  8369 Green — 1 skein

Method

To trace on design

Trace outline of heart onto tracing paper, cut out shape then pin onto blanket's centre. Baste around using fine sewing cotton to give you your guide line for embroidery placement. Repeat with bow at top of heart.

Repeat process for corner and 12 cm (5″) in from each edge.

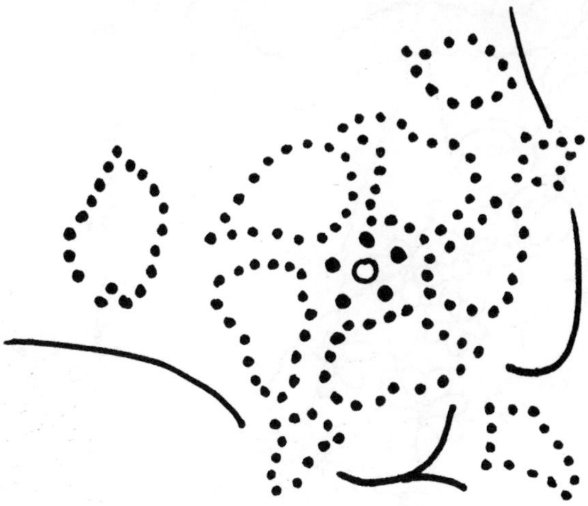

Blue Straight Stitch
Yellow French Knot
Lilac Chain Stitch
Lilac Straight Stitch
Lilac Straight Stitch
Ecru Straight Stitch
Blue Stem Stitch
Green Open Fly Stitch
Pink French Knots
Pink Lazy Daisy
Green Straight Stitch
Green Fly Stitch
Yellow Bullion Stitch
Yellow Bullion Stitch

HEART

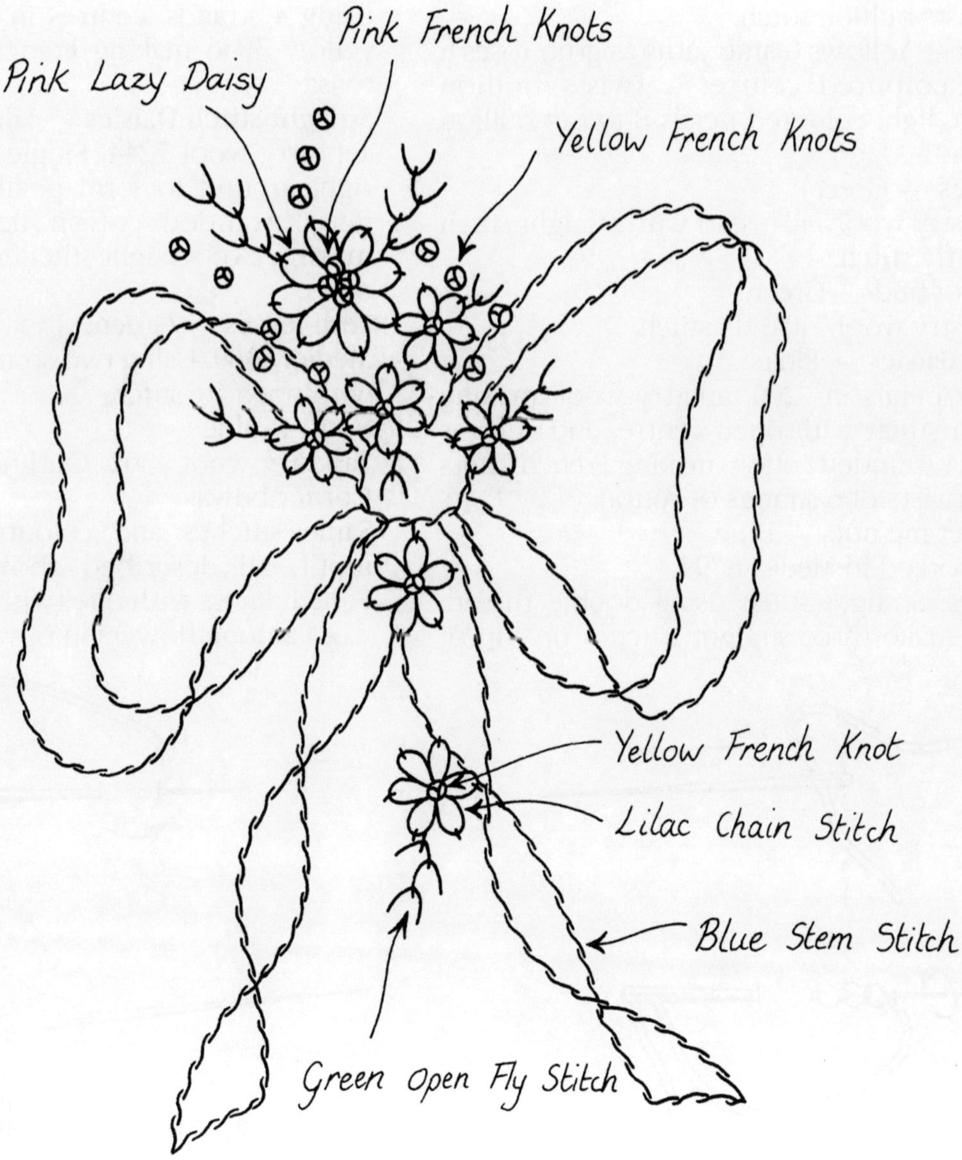
Pink French Knots
Pink Lazy Daisy
Yellow French Knots
Yellow French Knot
Lilac Chain Stitch
Blue Stem Stitch
Green Open Fly Stitch

Bow

Embroidery instructions

Grub roses — Yellows:
Dark-coloured centre from 7503 tapestry wool, light-coloured petals from 7745 tapestry wool.
Make centre 6 twists bullion stitch, petals 8 twists bullion stitch.
Buds — Yellows (same yarns as grub roses):
Dark-coloured centre, 4 twists bullion stitch, light-coloured petals 8 twists bullion stitch.
Leaves — Green:
Tapestry wool 7404, start with straight stitch then fly stitch.
Leaf of bud — Green:
Tapestry wool 7404, fly stitch.
Pink daisies — Pinks:
Work petals in 7200 tapestry wool, making chain stitch with open centre, and centres in 224 stranded cotton, making French knots of 2 twists of 6 strands of cotton.
Forget-me-nots — Blue:
All worked in Medici 8799.
Petals: Straight stitch using double thread. First make three straight stitches on top of each other using same holes, then make one straight stitch to lay either side, still using the same holes.
Chain-stitch Daisies — Lilac:
Stranded cotton 3042. Petals in chain stitch using 4 strands, centres in stranded cotton yellow 3046 making French knots using 1 twist.
Straight-stitch Daisies — Lilac:
Tapestry wool 7244. Single straight stitches right around to form petals, centres from Ecru stranded cotton using 6 strands, making two straight stitches on top of each other.
Fern leaves — Green:
Medici 8369. Using two strands, make leaves with open fly stitch.
Bow — Blue:
Tapestry wool 7302. Outline in stem stitch.
Corner bows:
Same stitches and colours as for centre motif, all described above. Add yellow French knots with one twist in 7745 tapestry wool among flowers in bow.

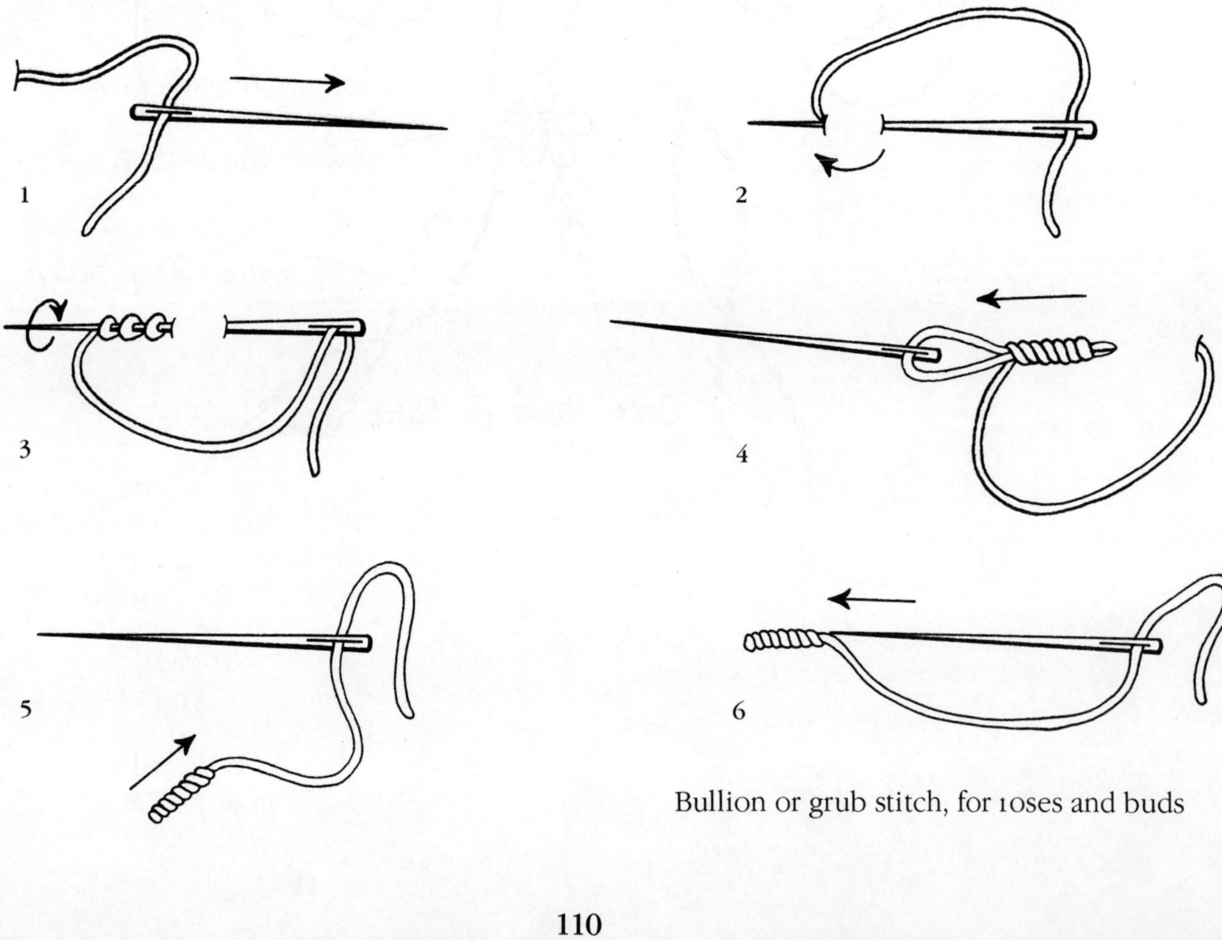

Bullion or grub stitch, for roses and buds

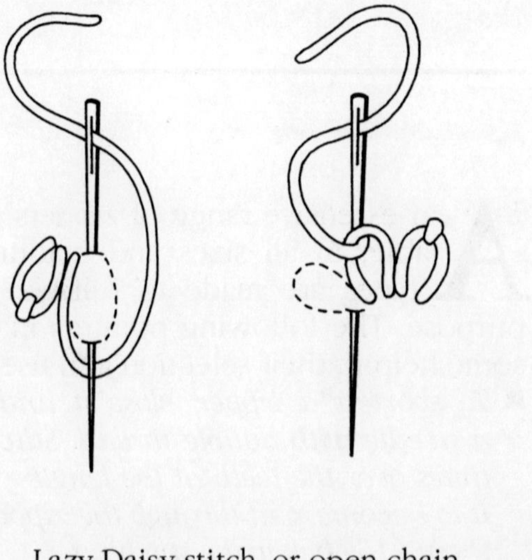

Lazy Daisy stitch, or open chain

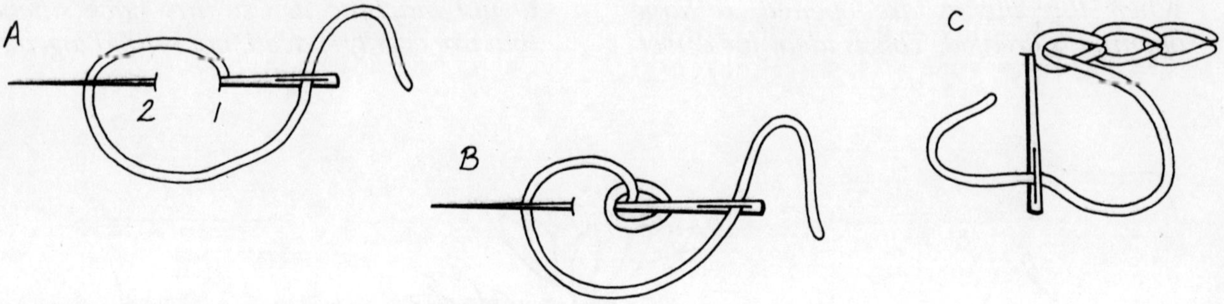

Chain stitch

To make up embroidered blanket

Place face down on a towel-covered ironing board and steam with light pressure only. Allow to cool. Place backing fabric across back of blanket and baste into place, trimming edges to be even with blanket. Apply blanket binding, or turn edges to back 1.5 cm (⅝′′) and baste, then stitch over entire hem depth with blanket stitch, keeping stitches 5 mm (¼′′) apart.

Zippers

An extensive range of zippers is available, in all sizes and colours. Most types are made to fulfil a specific purpose. The following pointers may be of some help in their selection and use.

- *To shorten a zipper, close it and thread a needle with double thread. Stitch many times over the teeth at the length you wish it to become. Cut through the zipper about 2 cm (1") below the stitching.*
- *If you cannot find continuous zipper (sometimes difficult to track down) purchase two of the longest zippers you come across. Position them with the pull tags adjacent in the centre of the opening. When the zippers are opened, a large opening is created. This is ideal for duvet-cover openings, or sofa covers, where the insertion space needs to be sizeable.*
- *If metal zippers are difficult to slide, rub a pencil lead over the teeth to help free the pull tag.*
- *Always use a zipper that is strong enough to do the job. Don't ask it to perform beyond the capacity for which it was designed.*
- *A hand-inserted zipper is the mark of a true designer finish to a garment. Using double thread (thread the needle with the end that first comes off the spool — thread tangles less this way) and a sharp needle, stitch in the zipper in the same way as you would machine it. Use tiny back stitches that are evenly spaced, not butted together.*